BITS, BRIDLES & SADDLES

BITS, BRIDLES & SADDLES

Doris Culshaw

B.T. Batsford Ltd • London

First published 1995

Printed in Great Britain by Butler and Tanner Ltd, Frome

Published by
B.T. Batsford Ltd
4 Fitzhardinge Street
London W1H 0AH

A catalogue record for this book is available from the British Library

ISBN 0 7134 7134 4

CONTENTS

Acknowledgements   6
Preface   7

Part 1 Bits

1   Snaffles   10
2   Snaffles allowed in competition   18
3   Snaffles, gags and mouthing bits   24
4   Pelhams   32
5   Double bridles   40
6   Conformation, action and temperament   50
7   How the horseman affects the horse   59
8   Problems with bitting   65

Part 2 Bridles and saddles

9   Nosebands, martingales and gadgets   74
10   Bridles and related items   87
11   Saddles and related items   93

12   Side saddles   102
13   Care of saddlery   107
14   Problems with saddling   112

Part 3 Horse and rider clothing

15   Riding clothes   116
16   What to wear   124
17   Safe clothing for stable work   128
18   Horse clothing   132
19   Outdoor rugs   137
20   Protective clothing for travelling   140
21   Protective boots for horses   143
22   Other tack   145

Glossary   152
Bibliography   155
Equestrian Suppliers and Services   156
Index   158

ACKNOWLEDGEMENTS

My interest in bitting was first encouraged by the late Major H. Faudel-Phillips. In later years Baron Hans von Blixen-Finecke made one understand that it was the whole of the horse that had to be understood, not just the mouth. My thanks are due to Ann Warr and Sandra Griffiths for their help in producing this manuscript, and to Vanessa Britton for her guidance.

PREFACE

It is essential to understand the correct use of bits, saddlery and artificial aids if we are to achieve harmony with our horse. It is our responsibility to the horse to make certain that what we ask of him is physiologically possible.

We must ensure that the horse will suffer no discomfort and that he will understand what we wish of him. By correct riding and schooling of the horse, we strengthen the horse's physique and keep him supple. If we do this, we can have a happy partnership with him for many years.

We must endeavour to improve our riding skills and knowledge at all times.

Xenophon, 430-355 BC, a gifted author, soldier and philosopher, wrote:

'It is not the bit but its use that results in a horse showing pleasure, so that it yields to the hand; there is no need for harsh measures; he should be coaxed on so that he will go forward most cheerfully in his swift paces.'

Part 1
BITS

1
SNAFFLES

Snaffles are undoubtedly the largest group of bits in use today, with an assortment of designs extending from the very kind to the most strong. The severity and action of any snaffle depends on the construction of its mouthpiece and the design of the bit cheeks, or rings. As a rule, the thicker the mouthpiece the more kind it is, because it has a broader bearing surface on the bars of the mouth. However, the conformation of each horse's mouth must always be considered. For instance, a fine Arab horse with a narrow mouth might find a thick mouthpiece uncomfortable. When considering a bit for your horse, assess the comfort of a mouthpiece by slipping your fingers between the bars while your horse's mouth is closed. If you can only get one finger in, then your horse certainly needs a bit no thicker than this, whereas if two or three fingers are easily admitted, then the choice concerning thickness is limited only by how severe you want the bit to be. However, always bear in mind that a mild bit can be made severe by rough riding, so strong bits should never be used by heavy-handed riders or by beginners who have not yet learned the degree of finesse required to use such bits accu-

rately. Having decided upon the severity of the bit, the next thing to consider is its action in the mouth, and on the rest of the head. The action of a bit is governed by the mouthpiece, the bit rings (or cheeks) and the horse's head carriage functioning in combination. Snaffle mouthpieces differ greatly in shape, thickness, materials used and overall construction, so the choice is not an easy one. Bit rings vary too, ranging from small, round, loose ring ones, to 'D' rings and full or half cheeks, so this makes the selection of a suitable bit all the more difficult. To help you make an appropriate choice, information on the various snaffles available and their intended uses is given in Chapters 2 and 3. In the following pages, the use of the word 'bit' is general, though it is also broken down to include snaffles, pelhams and curbs.

The action and fitting of snaffles

Snaffles are the easiest bit for a horse to understand and are used for basic schooling.

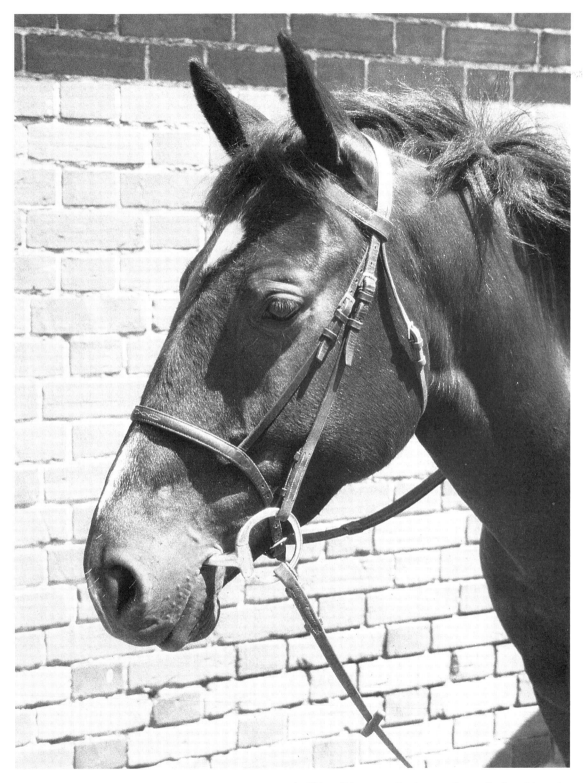

1a Too wide a snaffle which is fitted too low in the mouth. This will increase the 'nutcracker action' and tempt the horse to put his tongue over the snaffle

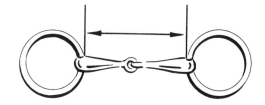

Fig. 1 A snaffle is measured inside the rings

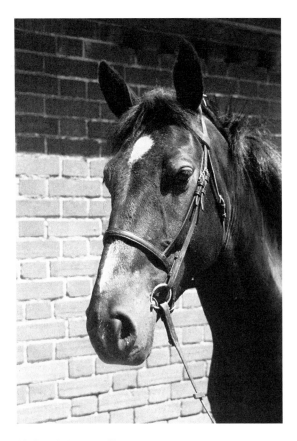

1b Too tight a snaffle

The action of the snaffle

The action of the snaffle is direct; no leverage is involved. In conjunction with the rider's forward driving aids, seat and legs and the use of weight, the snaffle indicates the direction of the movement. It also encourages the horse to have confidence in the rider's hands and to seek a contact with them.

The snaffle acts on the corners of the mouth, the bars and a little on the tongue. The exception is a straight bar snaffle which acts almost entirely on the tongue. The thicker the mouthpiece of the snaffle the milder it is, because it has a larger bearing surface than a thin snaffle. The fact that many snaffles are jointed and thinner towards the middle of the mouthpiece allows some pressure to be taken off the tongue.

Fitting of the snaffle

It is essential that the snaffle is the correct width for the horse's mouth. It is measured inside the rings of the snaffle. For most horses, snaffles between 11 cm ($4^{1}/_2$ in) and 14 cm ($5^{1}/_2$ in) are suitable.

Too wide a snaffle increases its severity because it increases the 'nutcracker action', pinching the corners and bars of the mouth between the two long branches of the snaffle. Also, too large a snaffle moves from side to side in the horse's mouth, which is highly uncomfortable because it brings the joint away from the centre of the mouth. The joint is designed to relieve pressure on the tongue, providing it is kept in the centre of the mouth.

A snaffle of the correct size should be adjusted so that when you pull the snaffle down it does not wrinkle the corners of the mouth, and only does so when you let go.

Have the snaffle on level holes on either side of the headpiece so that it will hang correctly. If it is on uneven holes the snaffle will work into a crooked position.

Putting on the bridle

Great care must be taken when putting on a bridle, otherwise it can be uncomfortable for the horse and he may become difficult to bridle. Have the bridle already adjusted to what you think will

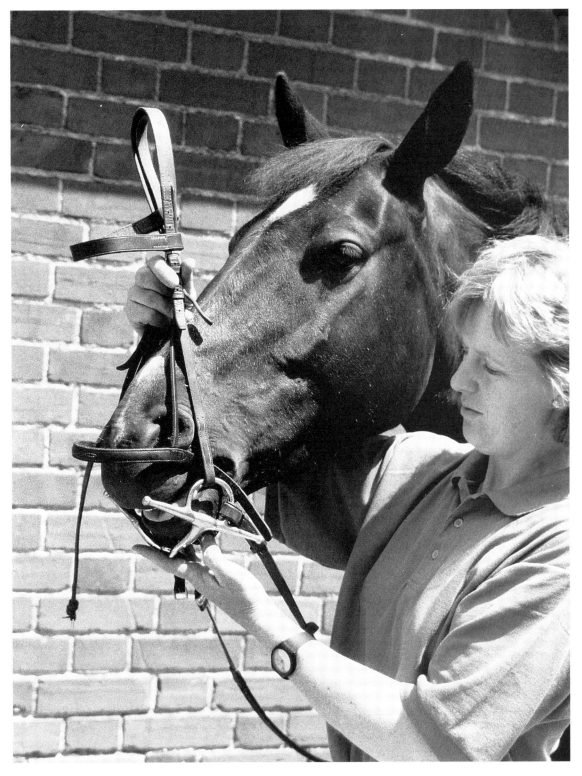

2 Putting on the bridle. Hold the horse's nose with the right hand. The left hand has the snaffle lightly held by the fingertips, while the thumb, inserted between the horse's lips, encourages him to open his mouth

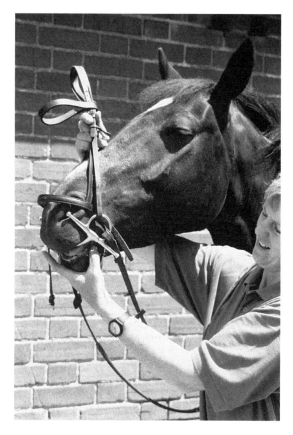

3 Slide the bit into his mouth

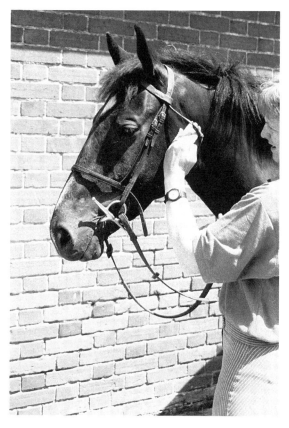

4 Fitting the throat lash. Allow a hand's width between the cheek and the throat lash

be the required size, with runners and keepers undone.

Hold the bridle over the horse's nose with your right hand. Your left hand holds the snaffle lightly by the tips of your first and second fingers, while your thumb is inserted between the horse's lips, encouraging him to open his mouth. When he does so, quietly slip the snaffle into his mouth and put his ears between the headpiece and browband one at a time.

If you push the snaffle against his teeth to make him open his mouth, he will be very unenthusiastic!

When you adjust the headpiece, do ensure that you take the time to give him a comfortable parting. If necessary, trim a one-inch section to make a 'bridle patch'. It is highly irritating for the horse if his mane is a tangled mess under the headpiece. When fastening the throat lash, allow a hand's width between the cheeks of the horse and the throat lash. If it is too tight, it will possibly deter him from flexing correctly.

A cavesson noseband is adjusted to allow two fingers at the side of the horse's head below the projecting cheek bones, and two fingers between the front of his nose and the noseband. Sometimes nosebands are fitted more tightly (see page 74).

The browband must not interfere with the hang of the bridle. When the bridle is fitted, just stand in front of the horse and make sure that the browband, noseband and the bit are all level and straight.

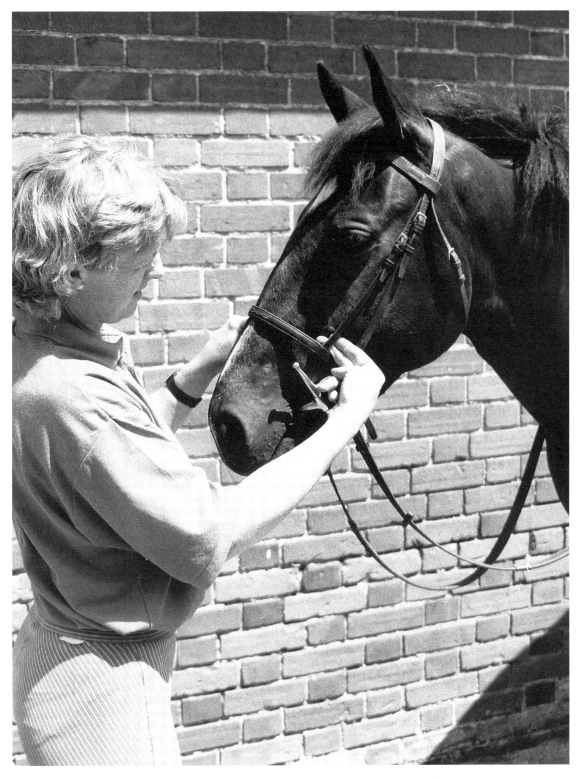

5 The cavesson noseband is adjusted to allow two fingers at the side of the horse's head below the projecting cheek bones

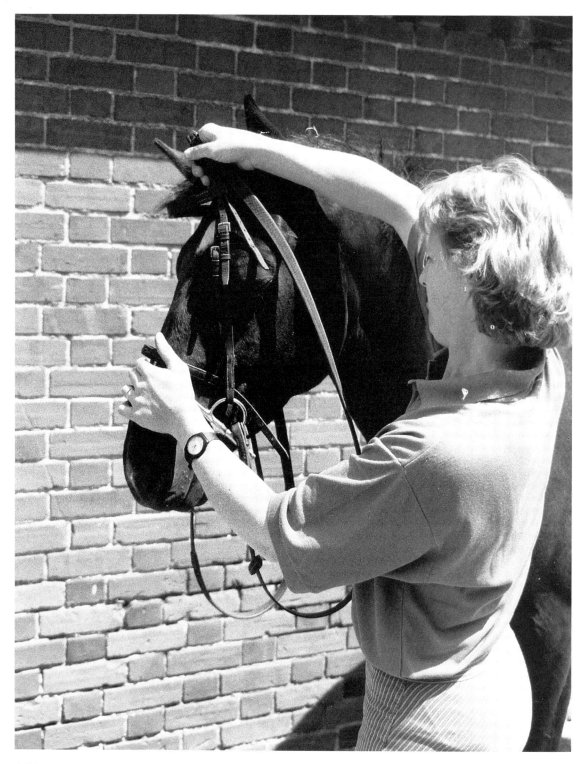

6 Taking off the bridle. Undo the noseband and throat lash. With the left hand steadying the horse's nose, the right hand gathers up the reins and headpiece, and slides them over the horse's ears and down his face. The left hand steadies his nose to prevent him throwing up his head

Taking the bridle off

Make sure that the horse cannot escape: have a headcollar around his neck and the rope through a haystring loop but not tied. If the horse should panic and rush back, the rope slips through the loop and does not frighten him; you will rapidly be able to grab the rope before he escapes.

First undo the throat lash and nose-band.

With the left hand steadying the horse's nose, the right hand gathers up the reins and brings them up to the head-piece. Quietly bring the reins and the headpiece over the horse's ears and down his face, allowing the horse to spit the bit out without it banging on to his incisors.

It is unkind to take the bridle off carelessly, banging the bit against his teeth.

Ensure that by correct fitting, the snaffle is as comfortable as possible for your horse, otherwise it will distract him and cause him distress.

Stainless steel

This is the safest and kindest metal for the snaffle. It is strong and does not wear, and it is easy to keep clean.

Nickel

While it may be cheaper to buy than stainless steel, it is unsafe. It wears quickly and can become very sharp where the rings go through the mouth-piece. Nickel is a soft metal and will bend and sometimes break without warning.

Some very cheap bits are made of plated steel and are a very bad buy. They do not last: the plating comes off and they become pocked with rust and are unsuitable for use. To spot a cheap plated bit, look at the joints and where the rings go through the mouthpiece (or in the case of an eggbutt snaffle, the ends of the eggbutt). Even in a new snaffle there will be small tell-tale signs of the steel underneath, or even of rust.

Summary

- The snaffle must be the correct size.

- It must be fitted correctly.

- The thicker the mouthpiece, the milder the snaffle.

- The snaffle is an easy bit for the horse to understand.

2
SNAFFLES ALLOWED IN COMPETITION

Competition snaffles

This chapter lists those snaffles that are allowed in BHS and FEI dressage competitions.

German hollow mouth loose ring snaffle

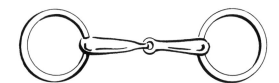

Fig. 2

A thick hollow bit. Being hollow, it is light and this is appreciated by the horse. The thick mouthpiece has a large bearing surface on the bars of the mouth and is less severe than a thin mouthpiece. Most horses go well in this snaffle; they like to move it up and down a little with their tongue, which the loose rings allow.

Eggbutt snaffle

The eggbutt sides prevent the snaffle rubbing the corners of the horse's mouth.

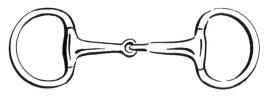

Fig. 3

These snaffles sometimes have a hollow mouthpiece, which is kind to the horse. They can also be solid and therefore heavier. Those with a thin mouthpiece are fractionally more severe. The mouthpiece may also be rubber-covered.

Flat ring snaffle

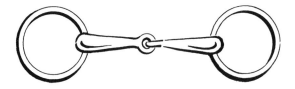

Fig. 4

This has a fairly thick mouthpiece. Horses go well in it because they can move it up and down with their tongue. It may rub the corners of the horse's mouth, although this is unlikely if the bit is made of stainless steel.

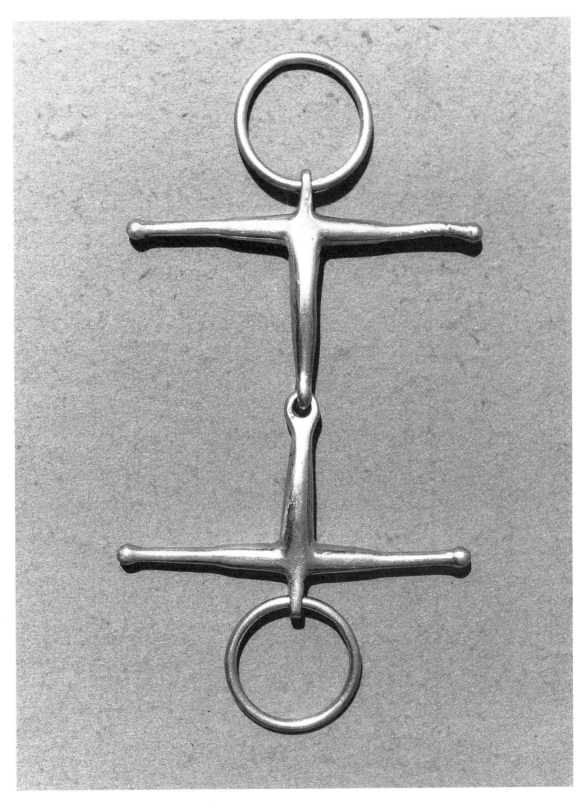

7 Fulmer, or Australian loose ring, snaffle

The Fulmer or Australian loose ring snaffle

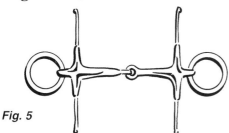

Fig. 5

The thick mouthpiece makes this a mild and comfortable snaffle. Designed with the loose rings on the outside of the cheeks, it gives a very clear turning aid and there is no chance of the snaffle rubbing the corners of the horse's mouth. The cheeks will help to teach a young horse to turn, in conjunction with the rider's leg and weight aids. Keepers attached to the upper cheek hold the mouthpiece up and straight, so there is less likelihood of a young horse getting his tongue over the bit. It is a heavy snaffle: some horses tend to take too much support from the bit and lean on it.

Cheek snaffle

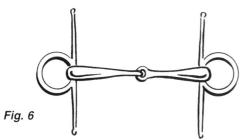

Fig. 6

Useful for young horses. In the case of severe resistance from the horse it will not slide through the mouth. It helps a young horse to understand the turning aid. It must be used in conjunction with the rider's leg and weight aids. It is not as heavy a snaffle as the Fulmer.

Spoon cheek snaffle

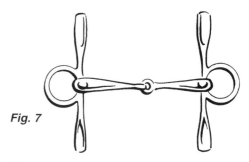

Fig. 7

This has the same attributes as the cheek snaffle. It is rarely seen on riding horses, but is frequently seen on 'trotters'.

Half spoon cheek snaffle

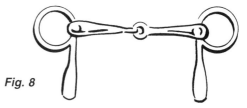

Fig. 8

Similar in action to the full spoon snaffle. In England, mostly seen on trotting horses.

'D' or racing snaffle

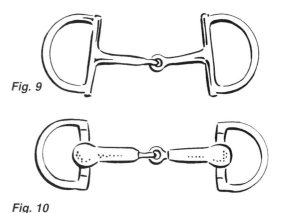

Fig. 9

Fig. 10

The 'D' cheeks help to turn the horse; the action is similar to that of the cheek snaffle. It may be covered in rubber, which makes it more acceptable in the early stages of schooling, and many horses go well in it. However, the rubber covering has a limited lifespan.

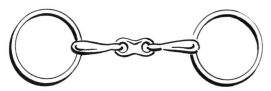

Fig. 11

French link snaffle

A mild snaffle, with a double joint. It is suitable for a horse that prefers very light pressure on its tongue. The French link may also have cheeks.

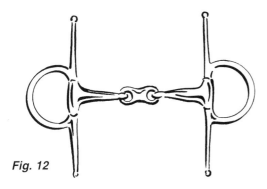

Fig. 12

'Dick Christian'

Fig. 13

Known also as snaffle with double joint or egg link. A very light bit, with a double link so there is less pressure on the horse's tongue. However, this snaffle is only made in a large size and is too wide for many horses.

Straight bar snaffle

Fig. 14

Fitted on the high side, it is useful for some young horses. They find it easy to understand. However, it acts mostly on the tongue and may encourage the horse to get his tongue over the bit.

Fig. 15

Rubber snaffles

Very mild, useful for young horses that are learning to accept the bit. It can only be used for very basic schooling. It may also be put on a horse when he is ridden by a novice, to save the horse's mouth. Another use for the rubber snaffle is to reassure a horse who is afraid for his mouth due to bad riding. A thin chain runs through the mouthpiece as a safety feature, in case the rubber is chewed through. These snaffles can be made of soft or hard rubber.

Vulcanite snaffle

Fig. 16

Similar in action to a hard rubber snaffle, but harder. If a horse chews on a rubber bit, a vulcanite snaffle is a suitable alternative.

Hanging snaffle

Fig. 17

This snaffle is designed to be straight in the horse's mouth and not drop in the middle, so there is less likelihood of a young horse getting its tongue over the bit. It would be more widely used if it were available with a thicker mouthpiece. It was designed by Baucher, a famous nineteenth-century riding master.

Nathe or Sprenger snaffle

Fig. 18

Made in Germany of pliable nylon. A mild snaffle useful for young horses that are learning to accept the bit and to become familiar with a contact. There are several differently-shaped mouthpieces. The most comfortable is the type with a tongue groove.

The disadvantage of these snaffles is that some horses will damage the mouthpiece relatively soon. For example, a horse with a highly strung disposition will, under stress, push the snaffle back with his tongue on to his molars and chew the mouthpiece.

It is as well to try the snaffle you think will suit your horse. Much depends on what you expect of your horse and your capabilities as a rider. Do not be afraid to experiment and to try a different snaffle: this can sometimes 'refresh' the horse's mouth. However, too much swapping of bits will have a detrimental effect. The horse loses a sense of security and may learn to distrust any bit. Do not experiment if all is well, and only experiment after considering the horse's health and the rider's ability.

Summary

- Keep to simple snaffles.

- The German loose ring snaffle is clear to understand and is comfortable for the horse.

- Before riding in a dressage competition, check that the snaffle your horse is wearing is permitted under BHS or FEI rules.

8 Eggbutt snaffles, showing mouthpieces of different thicknesses

3
SNAFFLES, GAGS AND MOUTHING BITS

There are many types of snaffle on the market. Some are very severe, causing the horse pain and discomfort which will make him increasingly oppose the rider.

When retraining an older horse, you should try different snaffles to see which will help him to understand your signals. Couple the new snaffles with re-education to the aids.

Many horses will perform well in the dressage arena, but when it comes to cross-country work they need a change of bit to give the rider more control, for example a gag snaffle or a Dr Bristol with a flash or Grackle noseband.

Hunting is very exciting for the horse, and again you may have to resort to a more severe bit.

If you really have a problem controlling your horse, seek help – opposition from a horse is usually a rider problem.

Dr Bristol snaffle

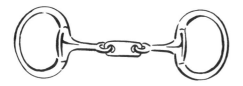

Fig. 19

Double-jointed severe snaffle. It has a thin mouthpiece and a flat spatulate middle section which is sharper and larger than the French link. This snaffle is useful for jumping and cross country riding, when a stronger snaffle may be needed. The Dr Bristol may have egg-butt, 'D' or wire rings.

Waterford snaffle

Fig. 20

A snaffle that is very mobile in the horse's mouth. This mobility discourages the horse from setting and crossing his jaw. This can be useful for a horse that sets his jaw or is very strong when jumping or going cross country. In the wrong hands it would be severe.

Cherry roller snaffle

Fig. 21

Not as mobile in the horse's mouth as the Waterford, it is used mostly with horses that have learned to set themselves against the rider. The rollers, which act on the corners of the mouth, the tongue and the bars, only become comfortable for the horse when he no longer resists the rider and relaxes his jaw. In good hands it has its uses for jumping and cross country.

9 Twisted snaffle (top); twisted nylon straight bar snaffle (middle); jointed cherry roller snaffle (bottom)

Magenis snaffle

Fig. 22

This is severe, having a square mouthpiece with rollers enclosed. Used carefully it will teach a strong, badly-schooled horse to respect it and not to set his jaw.

Scorrier or Cornish snaffle

Fig. 23

Very severe with a square mouthpiece, sometimes serrated. The inside rings attach to the headpiece and the reins to the outside rings. By its design there is more pinching or 'nutcracker action' on the horse's mouth.

Roller mouth 'D' snaffle

Fig. 24

The mouthpiece is made of alternate rings of stainless steel and copper, encouraging the horse to have a wet mouth.

Wire-covered 'D' snaffle

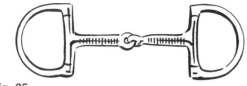

Fig. 25

Not a good snaffle: this could soon damage a horse's mouth.

Twisted snaffle

Fig. 26

Very severe, this too could damage a horse's mouth. The author would never use one.

Wilson snaffle

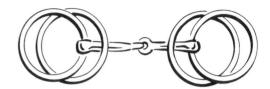

Fig. 27

Used mostly for driving. The inside ring is attached to the headpiece and the reins to the outside reins. By its design it has more pinching 'nutcracker action' than an ordinary snaffle.

10 A double mouth, or 'W', snaffle (top); Magenis snaffle (bottom)

Double mouth snaffle (commonly known as 'Y-mouth' or 'W-mouth' snaffle)

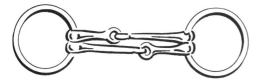

Fig. 28

This has two mouthpieces with the joints uneven. Severe and uncomfortable for the horse. While it may have a stopping effect for a short time, a horse will soon fight it and become very stressed.

Mullen mouth snaffle

Fig. 29

The mouthpiece is half-moon shaped. Useful for basic schooling, it has slightly less pressure on the tongue and slightly more on the bars than the straight bar snaffle.

Fillis snaffle

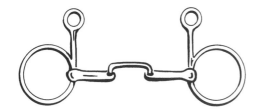

Fig. 30

A hanging snaffle with joints on either side of the port. There is virtually no 'nutcracker action' and there is plenty of room for the horse's tongue. Could be helpful for retraining a horse that gets its tongue over the bit.

Chain snaffle

Fig. 31

Very mobile in the horse's mouth, it is difficult to get a proper contact with it. It could be very severe.

Continental snaffle or Dutch gag (also known as a Belgian snaffle)

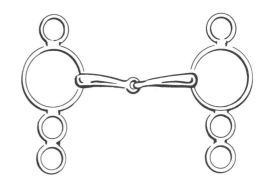

Fig. 32

This may have a stainless steel or nylon mouthpiece. With the bubble rings, the headpiece is attached to the top ring and the rein to the lower rings. The lowest gives the greatest leverage. It has a little action on the poll and has a gag-like effect. Its advantage over a gag is that the moment the rider 'gives', this is transmitted immediately to the horse –

he understands what is required of him, whereas some gags do not 'give' instantly. Useful for jumping when a stronger snaffle is required. By fitting the headpiece to the large snaffle ring, there will be no poll pressure.

Gag snaffles

These are snaffles that work by leverage. The bit slides up a rolled piece of leather or cord when pressure is put on the reins. Gags also have considerable pressure on the poll. The upward pressure is the greater and so the horse's head is raised. If the gag is used too much, the horse may bear down on it and evade it by becoming over-bent. In other cases it may cause the horse to go 'hollow'. Gags have their place but must be used with care.

The mouthpiece can be jointed rubber-covered, straight bar or rubber-covered straight bar. The larger the rings of the gag, the greater the leverage and poll pressure.

Always make sure that the holes through which the rounded leather or cord works are large enough to ensure a quick release of pressure when the rider 'gives'. Cord is better than rounded leather because it slips through the rings and 'gives' quickly.

The lateral effect of an ordinary rein attached to the ring of the gag can be advantageous for cross country work as it helps with steering. The gag working upwards with leverage does not give such a clear turning signal.

It is correct, safer and kinder always to use two pairs of reins, one on to the gag and the other on to the bit rings as

11 A gag snaffle in action, with the secondary rein attached to the rings of the gag

normal. This allows the leverage action to be brought into play only when necessary, and so is more effective.

The use of the gag is best kept for occasions when the horse is keener and apt to take charge, such as jumping and cross country work. By doing his everyday schooling in an ordinary snaffle you will help to educate him and not familiarize him with the gag, thereby preventing him from learning evasions.

A gag may be made from any snaffle

by using an over-rein. An over-rein is a longer rein than usual, made either of leather or of webbing. It goes through the nearside snaffle inside to outside, over the poll down the offside of the horse's head, through the snaffle ring outside to inside both reins, back to the rider's hands and buckles together. Using an over-rein allows you to try the effect of a gag on your horse before going to the expense of buying one.

Balding gag

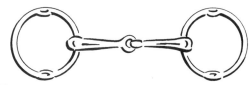

Fig. 33

Has large loose rings.

Cheltenham gag

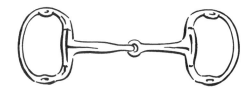

Fig. 34

Eggbutt rings.

Duncan gag

Fig. 35

Has slightly less poll pressure than the balding and Cheltenham gags. Designed to form part of a double bridle.

American gag

Fig. 35

Similar in action to the Continental snaffle.

Mouthing bits

Mouthing bits have keys, or players, to encourage the horse to play with the bit and get a wet mouth. The keys tend to discourage the young horse from putting his tongue over the bit.

Straight bar mouthing bit

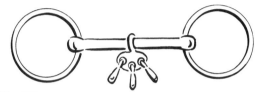

Fig. 37

This is the mouthing bit most commonly used. It must be fitted a little on the high side to lessen the chance of the horse getting his tongue over the bit.

Jointed mouthing bit

This design is uncomfortable for the horse. The ring in the middle presses on the tongue.

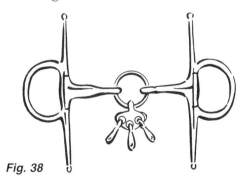

Fig. 38

It is becoming a less popular practice to use mouthing bits as they tend to make a horse 'fussy' in his mouth. Many people start a young horse off with a German hollow mouth snaffle or a rubber snaffle adjusted a little on the high side.

Tattersall ring bit

Fig. 39

Designed to have little or no pressure on the tongue. Not suitable for riding a young horse, it is used only for leading in-hand.

Whichever snaffle you decide to use on your horse, it must always be used in conjunction with your seat and leg aids. If you use hands only it will not influence the whole horse: it will be your hands against your horse's whole body. While a severe bit may check him for a while, he will fight it if it is always used and probably damage the bars of his mouth.

Summary

- If you are having a problem with your horse, do not resort to a more severe bit.

- Look to your own ability and get help.

- A severe bit can destroy a horse's confidence in the rider's hands.

- When changing your horse's bit, have regard for his and your capabilities.

4

PELHAMS

The pelham is a bit that combines the action of a snaffle with that of a curb but only has one mouthpiece. It was originally designed to satisfy the needs of riders who liked the control offered by a double bridle, but who did not want the hassle of using two bits (which had to be used with two sets of reins). Similarly, those who found snaffles inadequate for their needs often found that the pelham offered control without requiring the degree of precision needed to handle a double bridle. It is clear that although the pelham can be used with two reins, or only one if roundings are incorporated, it is a compromise between a snaffle and a double

12 Double link curb chain and jointed pelham with roundings

bridle, and so unavoidably its action is less precise than either of these.

The group of pelham bits has many designs which result from mixing the variety of mouthpieces attributed to snaffles with many of the cheeks and rings found on curbs. However, the cheeks of a pelham differ: an extra ring must be incorporated at the site of the mouthpiece on either side, in order to attach a 'snaffle' rein.

The theory behind pelhams is that you can ride off the snaffle rein until you require the action of the curb. To bring in the action of the curb you turn your wrist down and in, so that the curb rein makes contact with the bit and the horse then flexes at the poll. In reality, however, the majority of riders use roundings to join both bit rings together, so that only one rein need be used. Therefore both reins come into play at the same time, which results in the horse tucking his head in and thus bending his neck at some point behind the poll, rather than flexing as desired; this can result in the development of a ewe neck. Even if two reins are used, the action of the bit is still confusing to the horse, so it is not recommended for schooling. Nevertheless it does have its uses.

The pelham is often used when hunting to give a rider more braking power. It may restrain a child's pony that is rather strong for its small rider. It is also seen on show horses and ponies. To enable a rider to engage the snaffle action at any time, bringing the curb action into play only when necessary, a pelham should ideally be used with two reins.

Pelhams may be used with roundings so that the rider has only one rein to contend with, although its action will then be less precise. Alternatively an adjustable divided rein is available, which may be altered to bring more or less pressure on the curb.

Action of the pelham

The severity, or lack of it, is determined by the type of mouthpiece, the overall length of the cheeks and the adjustment of the curb chain. The longer the upper cheek, the more poll pressure; the longer the lower cheek, the more leverage can be applied and it therefore becomes a more severe bit.

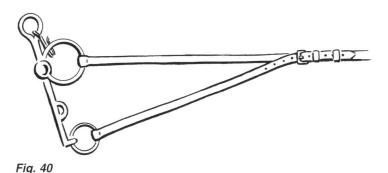

Fig. 40

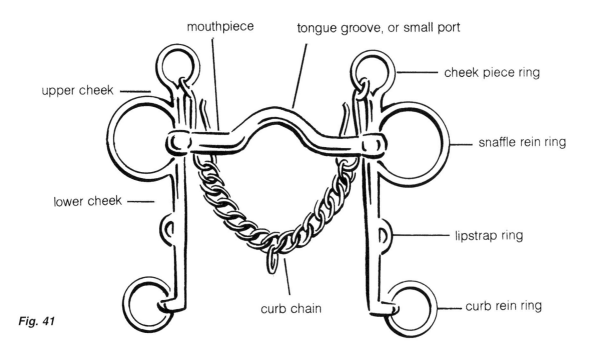

upper cheek ——

lower cheek ——

mouthpiece

tongue groove, or small port

—— cheek piece ring

—— snaffle rein ring

—— lipstrap ring

curb chain

—— curb rein ring

Fig. 41

Pelhams can be divided into three groups:

Weymouth action

The cheeks go through the mouthpiece and will act laterally. This means that when the reins are used, the cheeks turn out in that direction and help the horse to understand the signal. The Weymouth pelham may be slide mouth. The mouthpiece, sliding up the cheeks before it acts, helps the horse to understand the action of the curb. The horse has a brief warning that the curb is coming into action as the mouth slides up, and he learns to respond.

Fixed cheek pelhams

The cheeks and mouthpieces are fixed. There is no lateral action.

Banbury action pelham

The mouthpiece goes through the cheeks; therefore the cheeks work independently, and there is no lateral action. See also page 42.

Rugby link These provide the lateral action which is lacking in fixed cheek and Banbury action pelhams. Rugby links are sometimes also found on Weymouth action pelhams.

Fig. 42

Half-moon or Mullen mouthed pelham Designed to take pressure off the horse's tongue. However, this is not a succesful piece of equipment, because when the curb rein is used the mouthpiece turns and presses on the tongue. For this reason, horses do not go well in it.

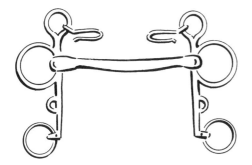

Fig. 43

Vulcanite pelham A thick, comfortable mouthpiece, this is one of the most widely-used pelhams. It is useful to give more control than a snaffle for hunting and cross country riding; also used on children's ponies.

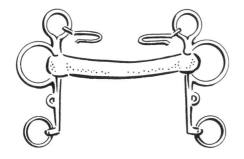

Fig. 44

Rubber pelham Comfortable mouthpiece which has a chain running through it as a safety factor. It can be made of hard or soft rubber; how long it lasts will depend on the quality of rubber. The hard rubber generally lasts longer. Similar in its action and use to the vulcanite pelham.

Jointed pelham Has a jointed mouthpiece. A fairly mild pelham: the joint takes pressure off the tongue.

Fig. 45

Arch mouth pelham The arched mouthpiece makes it suitable for a horse that does not like much tongue pressure or who has had an injury to the tongue.

Fig. 46

Hartwell pelham Has a small tongue groove to relieve pressure on the tongue.

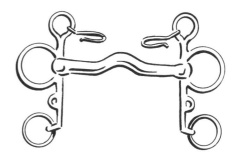

Fig. 47

Scamperdale The mouthpiece is bent so that there is no possibility of its rubbing the corners of a horse's mouth. The mouthpiece is a straight bar in action.

Fig. 48

Straight bar pelham Like the Scamperdale, this has more pressure on the tongue and bars than some of the other pelhams. One side of the mouthpiece may be serrated.

Fig. 49

Swales three-in-one The cheek pieces of the bridle attach to the rings of the pelham, as do the reins. There is no poll pressure and this pelham acts directly on the lower jaw. It is difficult to turn a horse in this bit, as there is no lateral action. The curb hooks are formed from part of the upper cheek. A very severe pelham.

Fig. 50

Hanoverian pelham The mouthpiece has cherry rollers on either side of a port. There are swivel joints on the lower part of the port, which makes the bit very mobile in the horse's mouth. A severe bit, sometimes seen on showjumpers.

Fig. 51

The Army reversible Originally designed to suit a large number of horses, the sliding mouthpiece of this pelham is liked by most horses. The mouthpiece is relatively thick with a comfortable tongue groove. It is called 'reversible' because one side of the mouthpiece is serrated and the other side smooth, so there is a choice between the smooth or the serrated side to the bars and tongue; the latter makes the bit sharper and more severe.

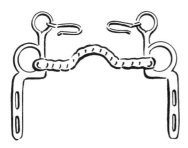

Fig. 52

The cheeks are designed with an 'elbow' for two reasons. First, a coltish young horse would find it difficult to catch hold of the cheeks with his teeth. Secondly, army horses on manoeuvres would be able to graze more comfortably during a rest with the 'elbow' cheek. The reins can be attached to the snaffle ring and either of the slots, the lowest being the more severe. It is sometimes used as the curb-bit of a double bridle. Still used by the Army and for police horses.

Rugby pelham A fixed cheek pelham either with a straight bar or with a mullen mouthpiece with Rugby links.

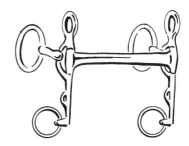

Fig. 53

Kimblewick This bit also has one rein. It has a small tongue groove. It is frequently used on children's ponies. Gives a little more control than a snaffle.

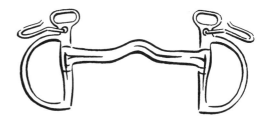

Fig. 54

Kimblewick with slots Putting the rein on the lower slot increases the action of the curb.

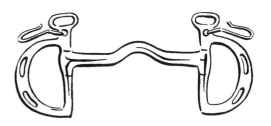

Fig. 55

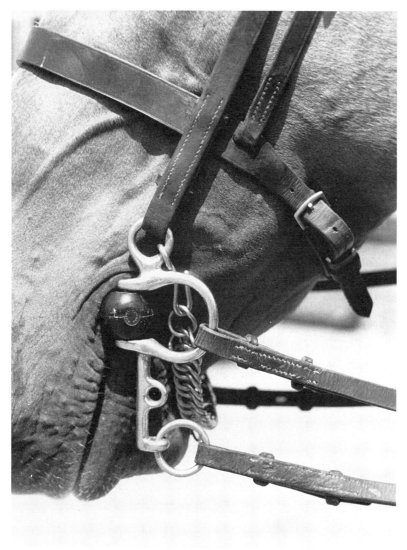

13 Pelham, with the curb chain inside the cheek of the pelham

The curb chain

There are two ways to put a curb chain on to a pelham.

The first method is to put it on the off-side hook, twisted clockwise until is is flat with the small fly ring at the bottom. If this ring is not at the bottom, take off the curb chain, turn it and once more twist clockwise until flat. The curb chain should come into action when the cheeks are at 45 degrees. If this is too tight, there is no play and the action will be severe. The horse responds better if there is a little play before the curb chain acts.

The second way to attach the curb chain begins as before: attach to offside hook, twist until flat, put it through the ring of the pelham across the curb groove and through the nearside ring and on to the curb hook. This way there is no possibility of the curb hooks rubbing the horse.

See also page 47.

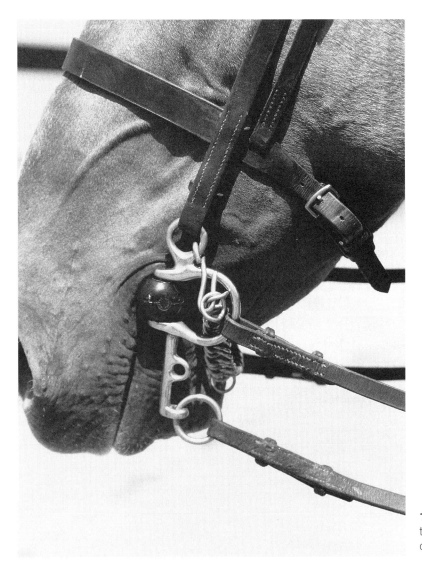

14 The curb chain passing through the rings on the cheeks of the pelham

Lipstraps

Most pelhams have a lipstrap. A lipstrap prevents the loss of the curb chain. With a Banbury action bit it controls the cheeks and stops them turning right over. The lipstrap is attached to the off-side cheek. It is threaded through the fly link and fastened to the short strap on the nearside.

Summary

- Pelhams are not to be recommended for the schooling of horses. They are difficult for the horse to understand fully.

- They may be useful on children's ponies to give the rider more control.

- In the hunting field they are used for the same reason.

- Do not be too quick to discard the pelham. It does have its uses.

5
DOUBLE BRIDLES

As its name suggests the double bridle has two bits. One is a curb together with a curb chain and the other is a snaffle, which used in combination with the curb is termed a 'bridoon'. The bridoon is a small version of an ordinary snaffle so that it fits in the mouth with the curb bit. As with other snaffles, the thicker the bridoon, the more comfortable it is. Similarly, as with other snaffles the bridoon may have loose or eggbutt rings and the mouthpiece may be single, or double-jointed. Types of curb bits are discussed on pages 42–46.

When handled by an educated rider the double bridle enables a high degree of lightness and accuracy to be obtained. The horse is ready to work in a double bridle when he is supple, balanced and working in collection. By such time the rider should progressively be taking more control of the horse through the legs and seat aids, and less through the reins. The rider should be sufficiently educated that he or she can use each of the bits independently. The bridoon is used to raise the horse's head and obtain 'lateral flexion', that is, to turn the head in the direction the rider wishes. The curb bit is used to encourage the horse to relax his lower jaw and obtain 'direct flexion', that is, to soften and flex at the poll. Should the bridoon be used without the curb, it would be practically impossible to obtain any degree of direct flexion; while using the curb without the bridoon will cause the horse to over-bend.

Once the horse has accepted the feel of both bits he can be expected to go forward into the bridle and not to withdraw from its action. Should this happen, it is a sign that the rider is not yet taking enough control through the leg and seat aids to use a double bridle effectively.

As well as the action of double bridles, their physical appearance is also important, as they are often used to enhance a horse's appearance in the show ring. A bridle designed for hunting or schooling may be made of strong, broad leather and this is also the correct type for heavy-weight show hunters. For horses that are shown in the light or middleweight categories, or in dressage, a medium weight bridle should be used. However, when showing ponies, hacks and even riding horses much finer leather is used, and it may also be prettily stitched.

One last consideration that should be given to the double bridle is the accessories that may, or may not, be used with it. The only noseband that should be used with a double bridle is a cavesson noseband, fitted above the bit (see page 74). Should any other noseband which incorporates a lower chin strap be used, it would interfere with the action of the curb chain and so confuse the horse. Whether or not you should use a running martingale with a double bridle is often a cause of debate. Some say you should never use one as you are already using a bit designed to lower the head. Others say that a running martingale attached to the curb rein offers double the action, should the horse raise his head too high. Obviously the use of a running martingale should be considered carefully in the light of individual circumstances and the experience of the rider. A standing martingale fitted to a cavesson noseband is acceptable, especially when used on jumping horses who are ridden in a double bridle. (For more information on martingales see Chapter 9.)

The action of the curb

The curb bit works by leverage, bringing pressure to bear on the bars of the mouth, the curb groove and the poll. The longer the upper cheek, the more downward pressure on the poll. The longer the lower cheek, the more leverage is applied to the bars of the mouth and the chin groove.

Bits must be the correct width. Too wide a mouthpiece will move about too much and the tongue groove will not be in the correct place. The mouthpiece is the correct width if it fits close to the outer surface of the lips without pinching.

Diagram of curb bit

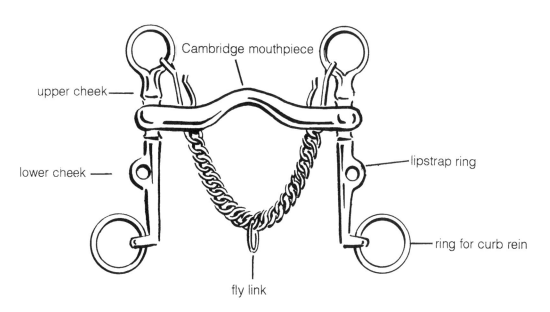

Fig. 56

Mouthpieces of double bridles

German mouthpiece

Fig. 57

Thick and comfortable. Always make sure that the tongue groove is sufficiently large to give the tongue some freedom.

Cambridge mouthpiece

Fig. 58

A popular mouthpiece, comfortable and with a sensible tongue groove.

Straight bar mouthpiece

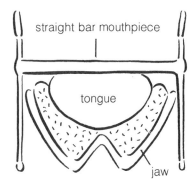

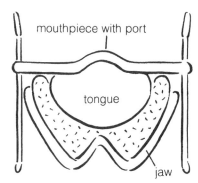

Fig. 59

Very rarely used, it has too much tongue pressure.

Arch mouthpiece

Fig. 60

Suits horses that cannot bear pressure on their tongue or that have had an injury to their tongue. Also more suitable for a horse with a coarse tongue.

Mouthpiece with a port

Fig. 61

No longer used: if it were too high it could act on the palate and be cruel.

Thinning

Fig. 62

(As found on a Banbury action bit.) Because the mouthpiece revolves, the thinning is the only feasible way of reducing tongue pressure.

Types of curb bits

Weymouth slide cheek

Many horses like the slide mouthpiece. They are able to move the mouthpiece a little and they find this comfortable. Some slide mouth cheeks have both a flat and a round side. Care must be taken when fitting a slide mouth to ensure that the flat side of the cheekpiece is to the inside.

With this bit, when the curb rein is

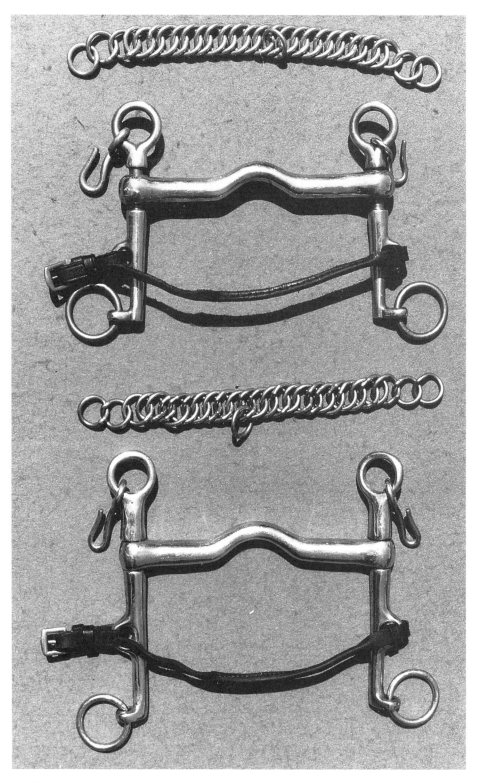

15 Slide mouth Weymouth bit, complete with lip strap (top);
Weymouth bit with no sliding action (bottom)

engaged the mouthpiece slides upwards; this gives more leverage. A horse is not slow to learn the effect of this action and that by flexing readily he will avoid the increased pressure.

Weymouth curb

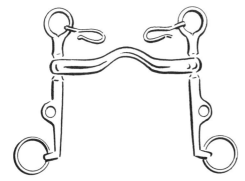

Fig. 63

No sliding action, therefore slightly sharper and more accurate, as no warning is given (which is the case with the slide mouth). The Weymouth curb illustrated has a very short upper cheek and so has very little poll pressure.

Fixed cheek curb

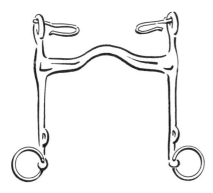

Fig. 64

The German curb bit is fixed cheek with a thick mouthpiece. The action of this bit is slightly more accurate than the slide

mouth. Used in dressage competitions. This German curb bit puts more pressure on the tongue. (See Fig. 57.)

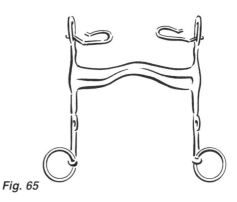

Fig. 65

Tom Thumb

A Weymouth action bit with very short cheeks and therefore less leverage. Useful for show ponies.

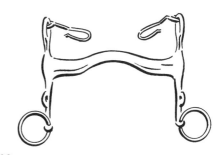

Fig. 66

Banbury action bit

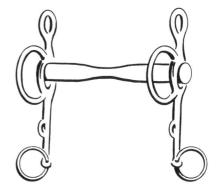

Fig. 67

16 A correctly-fitted double bridle

The revolving mouthpiece goes through slots in the cheeks. The cheeks therefore act independently. The pressure from the curb reins may not always be the same on either side. Thus the bit is not as sharp as those mentioned above, because one cheek may be acting more than the other. It was originally designed for horses with a one-sided mouth.

Globe bit

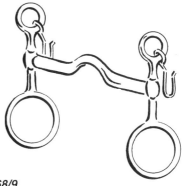

Figs. 68/9

45

Small curb bit with large rings for the reins. Used without a bridoon on show ponies when the young rider needs something more than a snaffle to show his pony off and can only cope with one rein.

Fitting a double bridle

Bridoon

Has its own headpiece, known as the 'bridoon carrier' or 'sliphead', which fastens on the offside. The bridoon should be fitted well up in the corners of the mouth like the fitting of a snaffle. It actually looks higher than a snaffle, because the bridoon rings are so much smaller.

The curb bit must be just below the bridoon and must be adjusted on level holes, otherwise it could work crooked.

To put it on, use the same technique as with the snaffle. Try the bridoon by the horse's head for size first, and adjust if necessary. Carefully hold both bits in two fingers of your left hand while your thumb encourages the horse to open his mouth.

Fig. 70

Fig. 71

Fig. 72

Fig. 73

17 The curb chain has been twisted clockwise until it is flat with the fly ring at the bottom

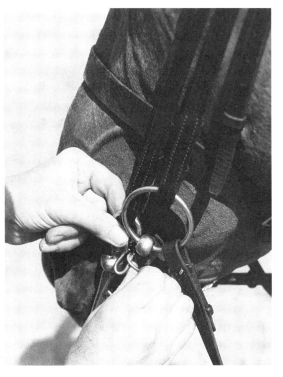

18 The chain is grasped and put on the hook thumb down

With the bits at the correct height, check that everything is straight: browband, noseband, bridoon level, curb level. This takes quite a bit of fiddling. Hold the cheek pieces of the bridle while you make sure the noseband is straight. Hold the noseband if you need to tweak the bridoon straight, and hold the noseband and bridoon carrier while you get the bit level.

Curb chains

The curb chain acts on the chin groove when the curb rein is used. It encourages direct flexion: if it is too tight there is no play. The horse will not understand and will possibly resist its action. Too loose and it is useless. The adjustment is correct when the curb chain acts with the cheek of the bit at 45 degrees to the horse's mouth.

Elastic curb chain (Fig. 70) The mildest of all. Can be used when a horse is first introduced to a double bridle. Useful when teaching students the use of a double bridle, until they are well practised at handling two reins. There is a tendency for them to ride too much on the curb, so the elastic curb chain eliminates this. The elastic curb chain has a small leather strap for the lip strap to pass through.

Leather curb chain (Fig. 71) Similar in action and usage to the elastic curb, but does not have the extra give. Has a small fly ring for the lip strap.

Double link curb chain (Fig. 72) Double links make for a smoother surface than a single link. Ideally the links should be wide so that they have a greater bearing surface. Narrow links are less comfortable for the horse.

Single links (Fig. 73) As long as the single links are wide and the chain is put on correctly and not twisted, single links are acceptable.

Rubber chain guard Threading the chain through a rubber guard makes the action less severe.

Fitting the curb chain

Put the chain on the offside hook and turn it clockwise until the chain is flat. Should the fly link be at the top, take off the chain, turn it over and start again. With the chain flat, make sure that it goes below the bridoon so that it does not interfere with its action.

Slide your fingers to the end link, fingers uppermost, and put the ring on to the hook, thumb down. The chain should then be flat.

If the chain is too long and just one link needs taking up, leave the end link on the hook, slide the second link up the inside of the curb hook and put the second link on top of it, still thumb down. This then looks like a double link.

Should the chain need to be shorter still, remove the chain, put the end link back on and put the third link on, again thumb down. This way the chain remains flat.

If the extra links are left hanging or are put on last, they may possibly work off.

Lip strap

Fastens through the fly link or, in the case of the elastic curb chain, through the leather loop. Its function is to prevent loss of the curb chain. With a Banbury action bit it prevents the cheeks from

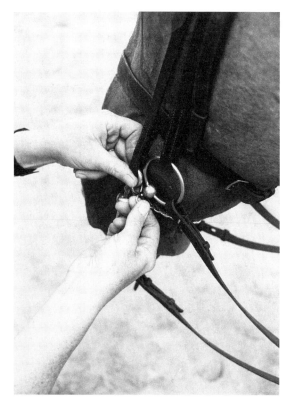

19 a The curb chain is shortened by one link. The first link remains on the hook

19 b The second link is slid up the inside of the curb hook and is placed on top of the first link

20 The curb chain is shortened by more than one link. Note that the end link is still on the hook and not dangling. The third link is put on thumb down

turning over. In no way can the lip strap be adjusted to affect the place where the curb chain lies.

Double bridles are used in dressage competitions from elementary upwards. Show hunters, hacks, riding horses and some show ponies are produced in them. They look smart and well turned out, and horses are usually schooled to go well in them.

Double bridles may be used to give more control in jumping competitions. For the same reason they are sometimes seen in the hunting field.

Summary

- Ensure that your double bridle is assembled correctly.

- Choose bits that fit your horse.

- The longer the cheeks of the curb bit, the more severe its action.

- A overly-tight curb chain eliminates the leverage action of a curb bit and it will be difficult for the horse to under stand.

6
CONFORMATION, ACTION AND TEMPERAMENT

The action of the bit and the horse's response to it depend on many things. Conformation, action, temperament, sex and breeding will all have a part to play, as well as the balance of the horse, his relaxation, suppleness and degree of schooling.

Conformation

A well put-together horse with a naturally well set-on head and neck will be easier to balance than a horse with a low set-on head and neck (that is, a large head or a short thick neck).

It is therefore important to acquire an eye for good conformation. The horse in photograph 21 has an elegant head that suits the horse and a good 'length of rein', which means a decent length of neck and a good shoulder. The head and neck are the horse's balancing pole, and he needs to have the freedom of his head and neck in order to adjust his balance. In time he will allow the rider to control these movements.

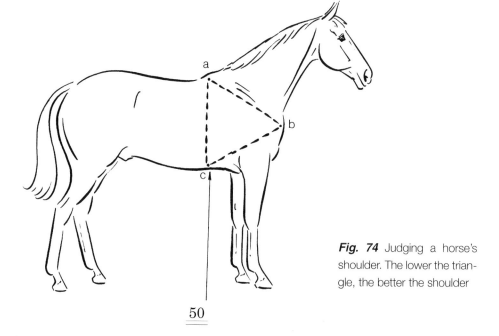

Fig. 74 Judging a horse's shoulder. The lower the triangle, the better the shoulder

To judge a good shoulder, imagine a triangle (as in Fig. 74) from the withers (a) to the point of shoulder (b), and from the point of shoulder to the girth groove (c). The larger the triangle, especially from (b) to (c), the better the shoulder.

Another guide to seeing a good shoulder is to look at the girth groove. The further back the girth groove, the better the shoulder.

The horse's middle piece should appear fairly square. In Fig. 75 you will see that A–B–C–D give the impression that the middle piece is compact and strong. A horse with a long, weak back and loins will have difficulty carrying the weight of a rider. In some cases a weak back will go hollow, that is drop and stiffen under the rider. This in turn causes

21 A good stamp of horse, with a well set-on head and neck

resistance to the rider's aids.

Looking at a horse's quarters (see Fig. 76), again imagine a triangle. As much length as possible from the hip bone (a) to the point of buttock (b) and to the stifle (c) is desirable. Length in all these sections means that the bone structure underneath can cope with the athletic qualities we demand from a horse.

The horse's leg needs to have an adequate amount of 'bone'. This is the measurement taken around the cannon bone, just below the knee (see Fig. 77). It needs to be at least around 20 cm (8 in) for greatest strength and the ability to carry weight. The shorter the cannon bone,

22 Horse with a low set-on head and neck, which makes her forehand heavy

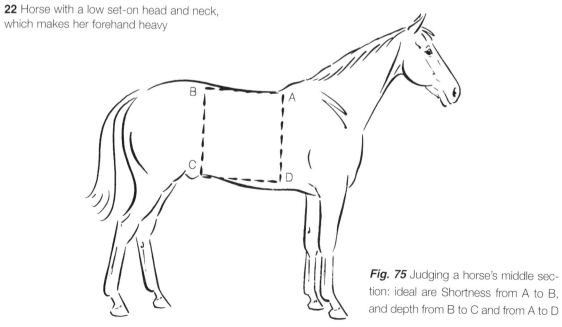

Fig. 75 Judging a horse's middle section: ideal are Shortness from A to B, and depth from B to C and from A to D

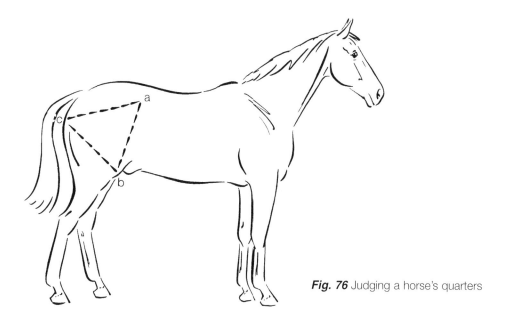

Fig. 76 Judging a horse's quarters

which is called 'well let down', the stronger the leg (see Fig. 78a). A long forearm – elbow to knee – allows for athletic action (see Fig. 78b).

The same applies to the hind leg. Short cannon bones and length from hip to hock are the features to look for. Hind legs that are 'in the next county' (Fig. 79) are difficult to bring under the horse to help him with his balance.

Ideally, the pasterns should have a similar slope to the shoulder. Too long a

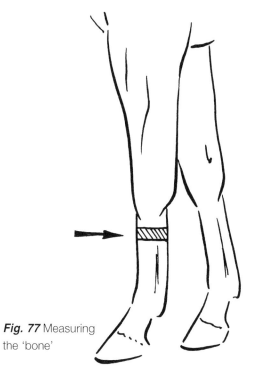

Fig. 77 Measuring the 'bone'

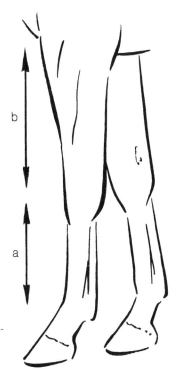

Fig. 78 Ideal proportions of leg

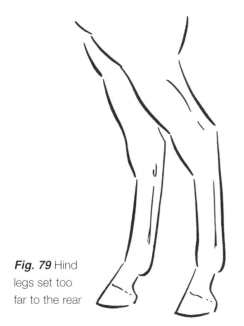

Fig. 79 Hind legs set too far to the rear

pastern is a weakness; upright pasterns, while stronger, do not absorb concussion so efficiently.

How the head is set on to the neck is important. There should be sufficient room (about two fingers) between the jawbone and the atlas bone. Also the

Fig. 80 Judging a horse's head and neck (two fingers between jaw and atlas bone)

width under the jaw bones should be ample. Horses that have a good width between the lower jaw bones also have more freedom to flex.

The structure of the mouth should be understood. The bars of the mouth, on which the bit acts, are the part of the jaw between the incisors and the molars in a mare, and the tushes and the molars in a male horse. The bars are toothless areas, covered by a thin, sensitive membrane. The thinner and sharper the bars, found for example in well-bred horses, the more sensitive they are. In less well-bred horses the bars are thick and fleshy, and not so sensitive.[Fig. 81]

Bars can be damaged by misuse of the bit. The membrane will bruise. The periosteum covering the jaw bone can also become inflamed, damaged and calloused. In some cases a permanent lump can be felt on the bars.

With young horses every effort must be made not to damage their mouths and destroy their natural sensitivity. It may appear to the novice rider that a young horse has a 'hard' mouth – not so. He is simply uneducated in his mouth, mind and body.

In some breeds of horse, notably the Arab, the lower jawbones nearer to the chin groove are narrow. This leaves very little room for the tongue. Thus the tongue takes some of the pressure off the bars, and therefore with this type of mouth the tongue receives more pressure than many horses tolerate. Some horses have large tongues, which may be a problem (see page 65).

Balance

When you first ride a young or unschooled horse, your weight will upset his natural balance. He will initially try

23 This horse is built very much downhill, and will be more difficult to balance

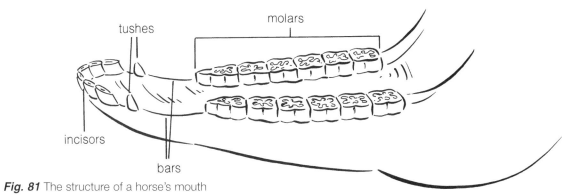

Fig. 81 The structure of a horse's mouth

24 This young horse has good conformation, with a decent length of stride. With correct work, his top line, i.e. along the top of his crest to his croup, will muscle up more

to carry most of your weight on his front legs. This is known as 'being on his forehand'. Through correct schooling he can be taught gradually to transfer more weight to his hindquarters. He will learn to step under more with his hind legs, and by using his hind legs and back he will lighten his forehand, so becoming balanced under the rider. The better bal-

anced the horse, the lighter the aids needed to control him.

Action

A horse with an athletic action will be easiest to school. He needs to have a good length of stride, using his shoulders well. The hock action should be very active. It is difficult to encourage a horse to improve his balance if his hock action is poor.

When viewing a horse from the front,

you should look for a straight action (and similarly from the rear). Trotting with legs too far apart, or too close, is undesirable. If they are too close, he may 'brush', or even hit himself with the opposite foot or shoe.

In no way must the rider or the action of the bit interfere with the action of the horse. One of the golden rules of good riding is that one must never spoil the horse's natural action.

Temperament

A forward-thinking horse will be easier to balance and to school than a dull and sluggish one. A very keen, or 'hot', horse will require great tact when being persuaded to accept the rider's leg and the bit. A generous temperament is needed, whichever discipline you have in mind. A generous horse is one that will cooperate willingly and try to do his best. When

25 An active trot, but the horse is not tracking up, nor is he stretching down on to the bit. The equipment is fitted well, although the cavesson would fit better had the noseband of the bridle been removed

26 A horse with a bold, kind eye

viewing a horse, the eye is the guide to temperament: a kind, bold eye is the one to look for. The ears are also a good indicator. A moody horse may have his ears back while simply standing in the stable.

Breeding

The better bred the horse, for example a thoroughbred or an Arab, the more responsive it will be to the rider's aids. This is because the connective tissue throughout the body is thinner and more sensitive, making the horse very perceptive to touch, and its reactions will be very much quicker.

Condition

The horse should be sufficiently fit to do the work required of him. An unfit horse's muscles will tire quickly, so he should be gradually built up both in condition and in work, so that he can work without stress. A tired horse – a horse in poor condition – may start to lean on the bit and so learn a bad habit.

Age

A well-schooled and supple horse will be pleasant to ride until he is quite elderly. Starting to school an uneducated older horse will not be as easy a prospect as dealing with a younger subject. His muscles will be set in the wrong shape and he will probably resent some of the schooling exercises, but with tact, sensitivity and careful bitting amazing achievements can be made.

While we may look for the ideal horse, in many cases we will have to do the best with what we have, always remembering the golden rule: comfort is the key to the horse's mouth.

Summary

- When choosing a horse, his temperament is of paramount importance.

- A naturally well-balanced horse will be easier to school than one with a low set-on head and neck.

- A horse with an athletic action will also be easier to school.

- With tact and skill, most horses will respond and improve their way of going.

7
HOW THE HORSEMAN AFFECTS THE HORSE

27 Note the straight line from the rider's elbow through the wrist to the horse's mouth. Ideally the rider's fingers should be closed around the reins; this gives the rider a better contact

The rider

The rider is a burden to the horse, and it is therefore every rider's responsibility not to impede him nor his way of going. The only way to achieve this is by sitting correctly, which means adopting a balanced and supple position. This enables you to follow and absorb the horse's movement. You will then be responsive to messages from the horse that are received through seat and hands. Your feel for the horse will enable you to time your aids and 'speak' clearly through them to the horse.

Hands

The position of your hand influences the action of the bit. The golden rule is to create a straight line from the rider's elbow, through wrist and hands, to the horse's mouth. The height at which the hands are carried is governed by the position of the horse's head and neck. If this line is present, there is neither upward nor downward tension and your hands are at their most agreeable to the horse.

28 Holding the reins of a double bridle: the rider's little finger divides the snaffle and curb rein

The reins

A horse's mouth is only as sensitive as the hands at the other end of the reins.The reins should be held held lightly by the thumb, to prevent slipping, right at the base of the fingers and then across the palm. The tips of the fingers are against the palm of the hand. Pressure is increased on the horse's mouth by turning the hand. Hands act, resist or yield. The length of rein must be so adjusted that the hands do not need to pull backwards. The correct length of rein will establish contact with the horse's mouth. The rider answers resistance with resistance and responds instantly to the horse by softening the fingers, elbows and shoulders, and conversely will answer to lightness with more lightness. The hands must feel animated and alive, never dead, heavy or set.

The hands must never pull. By pulling you only provoke resistance in the horse. The more you pull, the more strongly the horse will pull. No prizes for guessing who will win!

The unbalanced rider

An unbalanced rider will impede the horse, who will have to cope with an unbalanced object on his back, which in turn makes it difficult for him to balance himself. An unbalanced rider will have unsteady hands; at worst the rider may be keeping his balance by hanging on to the reins. If this is the case, the rider's signals to the horse will be harsh and may make the horse afraid of the bit. It will then be a difficult task to regain the horse's confidence. The horse will be behind the bit and will not want to seek a contact with the rider's hands. The horse may also come above the bit in an attempt to run away from the discomfort.

Stiffness in the rider

Any stiffness in the rider makes him sit more heavily than he ought, and out of harmony with the horse. Stiffness in the shoulders will make the hands harder. Stiffness also affects the rider's coordination of the aids, which in turn muddles the horse. Stiffness anywhere in the rider's body causes the horse to stiffen in turn against the rider. This causes the horse stress and impedes his ability to use himself correctly. The horse's action deteriorates. All this affects the horse's response to the bit.

Armchair seat

This is when the rider sits on the back of the saddle with his legs too far forward. This has the effect of making the rider land heavily on the horse's back, particularly in the rising ('posting') trot. In this position the rider is unable to use his legs correctly. He is therefore likely to be dependent on the rein aids alone in order to control the horse, as his leg and seat aids are ineffective. A rider in the 'armchair' position will probably resort to a more severe bit.

A perched position

A 'perched' position is when the rider sits on his fork with an unnaturally hollow back and probably rides with a length of stirrup leather too long for his capabilities. The perched position is very uncomfortable for the horse because the rider is unable to follow and absorb the movement of the horse. This sets up resistance in the horse which will be felt through his back and mouth.

Crookedness

'Crookedness' means that the rider is in the habit of slipping to the outside when riding through corners or in a circle, or that the rider may always sit on one side no matter which rein he is on. The crooked rider will use his weight aid incorrectly and his leg aid will be ineffectual on one side: if the rider slips to the outside, the inside leg will be shorter than the outside leg, thus making his inside leg very weak. This will not encourage the horse to bring his hind leg under him on that side. The one-sidedness will be felt in the horse's mouth. Some horses are known to throw a rider to one side or the other. If this is so with your horse, you must be aware of this and continually correct your weight and balance.

Knowledge

The rider must be educated to understand his influences on the horse: how to coordinate legs, weight, seat and hand aids and to apply them clearly and concisely. The rider must have an understanding of and feeling for what is implied by having the horse 'between leg and hand', and of riding 'from inside leg to outside aid'.

As a rider's knowledge and ability improve, so will the horse's response to

29 The rider is sitting on the back of her saddle with her legs too far forward: she will therefore be behind the movement of the horse

30 The rider is in too perched a position, with too long a stirrup for her capabilities

the bit and aids.

Any stiffness in the rider, one-sided-ness or bad position in the saddle sets up a resistance and stiffness in the horse. Again, this will be felt in the horse's mouth.

Only when the horse is calm and allowed to relax will he be in a state of mind to co-operate with his rider.

The rider, by sitting correctly and being supple, balanced and relaxed, allows the muscles of the horse to func-tion with little effort. It is very impor-tant that the rider remains supple and relaxed to be effective.

Usually, the bit that suits the horse depends on the ability of the rider. The more able the rider, the less likely he is to use severe bits.

We have a responsibility to the horse to understand his difficulties and to be fair to him by explaining clearly what is required of him.

Summary

- Continually seek to improve your riding ability.

- If you have a problem, get help from a qualified instructor.

- Have lessons on well-schooled horses and improve your knowledge and feel.

31 A very crooked position. The rider is slipping to the left and collapsing her right side

8
PROBLEMS WITH BITTING

Mouths

Horse's mouths vary in shape and sensitivity. The mouths of the thoroughbred and the Arab are the most sensitive and delicate of all.

The lips

The lips are not as sensitive as the bars. In some horses the lips stretch more than in others, and in this case there can be problems, as the bit presses the inside of the horse's cheeks against his molars.

Chin groove

The part of the horse's head we call the chin groove, or curb groove, also varies in sensitivity. Again, in the thoroughbred and Arab it is more sensitive. The chin groove is not as sensitive as areas higher up the jaw, where the skin is thinner. This must be borne in mind when fitting a curb chain. The curb chain, correctly fitted, can be comfortable, unlike one that acts in the wrong place. Nowadays we rarely find a curb chain too high up the jaw. Years ago, when curb bits had longer upper cheeks, it was common to find horses injured by their chains.

The tongue

The tongue varies in size. Some horses have quite a large tongue, while others of a comparable body size have smaller tongues. It must be remembered that the tongue is very sensitive, and, within reason, it must be allowed to move a little when bitted and not have a dead pressure on it.

Channel for the tongue

The channel, or lingual canal, also varies from horse to horse. Horses with a very narrow channel, in which there is insufficient width or depth for the tongue, must be bitted with care.

The nose

The cartilage of the nose is especially sensitive just where it joins the bone. Therefore this particular spot must be avoided when fitting a dropped noseband or a bitless bridle. You must ensure that the pressure is taken on the bone.

Injuries to the mouth

Sore corners of the mouth

Rubbing may be due to an excitable horse pulling and messing about.

A nickel snaffle will wear very sharp and damage the lips. Some bits nip the corners of the mouth; this can happen with Banbury action bits.

Should a worn nickel snaffle be the cause, discard it. The rubbed corners of the horse's mouth must be allowed to heal before another snaffle is used. If the horse must remain in work, either lunge it from a breaking cavesson or use a bit-less bridle. If you find that the corners of the horse's mouth are tender and have a tendency to be rubbed, use bit guards. See page 86 for a full description of rubber bit guards and their uses.

Bruising of the bars

Usually caused by bad riding, the horse is 'jabbed' in the mouth by, for example, a rider yanking on a loose rein. In extreme cases the bone can be damaged.

The horse must not have a bit in his mouth until all bruising has healed. If he is ridden with a sore mouth he will become upset and start to fight the rider.

To feel for bruising, gently run your thumb along the bars and compare both sides of the horse's mouth. Where there is damage there will be a soft thickening and tenderness. If the injury has been bad enough and the jaw bone has been damaged, you will feel a permanent hard lump.

Wolf teeth

If these interfere with the bit, your vet will have to remove them.

Lacerations on the inside of the cheeks

These are caused by the horse's cheeks being pressed on to sharp molars.

An over-large snaffle with excessive nutcracker action will cause this. Check that the snaffle is the correct size, and also have the horse's teeth checked.

Injury to the chin groove

Caused by an incorrectly-adjusted curb chain that has been put on twisted instead of flat.

The chin groove must be allowed to heal. Then use an elastic curb chain or a sheepskin-covered one. There are rubber covers for cheek guards for curb chains, but if they get wet with rain or sweat they tend to rub the horse.

When the horse is relaxed and giving his jaw confidently, you may return to using an ordinary curb chain, making sure it is correctly fitted (see page 47).

Injury to the tongue

Sometimes a foreign body in the feed can damage a horse's tongue.

Putting a rope through a horse's mouth and round his lower jaw will injure the tongue. This is sometimes done to restrain horses, and is not recommended.

How to examine a horse's mouth

Great care must be taken when looking into a horse's mouth. He can easily be upset and may possibly strike out with a foreleg. Put a headcollar on the horse and have him facing the stable door, which must be closed. First look at the external parts, that is the lips and chin groove. Stand on the horse's nearside, put your right hand under his jaw and hold his nose with your right hand. Gently feel the bars of the mouth with the fingers or thumb of your left hand, checking for any thickening or lumps. You may find wolf teeth, which are short rudimentary teeth with little root.

Then, holding the nose steady with one hand, carefully look inside the horse's cheeks for wounds or signs of old scar tissue.

To examine a horse's teeth you must be an expert. The novice could easily get his fingers nipped. The examination is best left to a veterinary surgeon or a horse dentist, who will examine the molars for sharpness, particularly the outside edge of the upper molars and the inside edge of the lower jaw molars. These can wear unevenly and become sharp. Young and old horses should have their teeth checked every six months. Other horses should be attended to yearly.

A 'parrot-mouthed' horse (whose upper jaw is overshot) can cause bitting problems. The incisor teeth are out of alignment, and so are the molars which then wear unevenly; a hook can form at the front part of the upper molars and the back of the lower ones. The hook on the part of the upper jaw can damage the inside of the cheeks when the bit is acting.

Regular rasping of a horse's teeth obviates these problems.

Evasions

Tonguing (getting the tongue over the bit)

Most commonly found in better-bred horses, for reasons stated earlier in this chapter, and in Chapter 1. It is very uncomfortable for the horse. All the pressure from the bit is directly on the bars and there is no cushioning effect from the tongue.

Causes Too large a snaffle. Pressure in the wrong place makes it very uncomfortable for the horse's tongue. A snaffle that is too large also drops down in the mouth and makes it easier for the horse to put his tongue over the bit. Fitting the snaffle too low in the early stages of schooling a young horse encourages this bad habit. Bad riding and hard, unyielding hands can also cause this habit.

To help the horse get over this bad habit, choose a thick, comfortable snaffle that fits the horse. Have ready a piece of soft string about 45 cm (18 in) long. Thread the string through the middle joint of the snaffle, put on the bridle with the string outside the horse's mouth, then bring the string up and tie it to the cavesson noseband towards the front. Have the noseband a little tighter than usual.

The string holds the snaffle up in the horse's mouth and lessens the likelihood of his getting his tongue over the bit. Then, most importantly, ride and school the horse correctly. It will take a little time because horses are such creatures of habit.

When you feel that the horse has learned to keep his tongue in the correct place, gradually loosen the string until he can be ridden without it. The horse may be more comfortable in a double-jointed snaffle which has little tongue pressure. A hanging snaffle may help, fitted a little on the high side. This design of bit does not drop down in the middle like an ordinary snaffle. A

32 A horse having his teeth rasped. The practitioner has a special gag in the horse's mouth to facilitate the rasping

Fulmer snaffle with keepers on the upper cheeks may help for the same reason.

Sticking the tongue out to one side

The horse lolls his tongue out when being ridden.

Causes The same as for tonguing.

This must be treated in a similar fashion as tonguing. Of the two evasions, this is the more difficult to correct. Again, correct riding is of major importance.

Drawing the tongue back

The tongue is arched so that air is sucked in.

Causes This is a stress-related problem. When the horse is worked in and relaxes, the tongue usually goes back to its proper place.

Crossing the jaw

The horse crosses his jaw and sets himself against the rider.

Causes Usually bad riding causes this problem.

First examine the mouth to ensure that there is no damage. A Grakle noseband will help, as long as one remembers that this is treating the effect and not the cause. The real answer is to get help from a qualified riding instructor.

Opening the mouth

When the rider resists with the reins, the horse opens his mouth instead of relaxing the lower jaw.

Causes Usually bad riding, possibly 'all hands and no legs' on the rider's part.

Check the mouth for damage. A dropped noseband helps but again is treating the effect and not the cause. Go to a good riding instructor for help.

Hard mouth

There is little or no response to the rein aids.

Causes The horse's mouth may be insensitive because he has never been taught to become responsive to the rider's aids. Stiffness throughout the horse's body is felt by lack of response to the rein aids. It is quite possible for a horse to be ridden by an uneducated rider for years and yet to be controlled to a certain extent. The horse's mouth becomes increasingly insensitive.

First, examine the horse's mouth for damage to the bars. There may be lumps or callouses, in which case there is not much to be done for him. A bitless bridle may help. Should there be no ascertainable damage, correct schooling may help to overcome a hard mouth.

A mouthing bit may help by encouraging the horse to play with the bit and get a wet mouth. Generally, the milder the bit you use with a hard mouth, the sooner the horse will respond. This is not a suggestion to put a hardened old sinner in a rubber snaffle and then take him hunting! He must be 'put to the aids' before there will be any benefit. *The Undisciplined Horse* by Ulrick Schramm is helpful on this subject.

One-sided mouth

The horse will be soft on one side but stiff on the other.

This is rarely a mouth problem alone. Years ago all sorts of bits were designed for a one-sided mouth, but it is now recognized to be a schooling fault. *The Undisciplined Horse* (Schramm) describes the problem perfectly, and how to correct it.

Tilting the head

When he is ridden, the horse tilts his head: one ear will be lower than the other.

First have your horse checked by a chiropractor. Then look to your riding and schooling of the horse.

Behind the bit; dropping the contact; overbending

Fig. 82 Going behind the bit

The horse bends his neck and poll and 'overbends', that is the head comes behind the perpendicular. In this way the horse drops the contact with the rider's hands and becomes difficult to control.

Causes Insensitive riding: rough hands making the horse afraid of the contact; or use of a sharp or severe bit.

Use a mild snaffle and endeavour to

ride it forward into a steady (not fixed) sympathetic hand. It will take some time for the horse to get confidence in the rider's hands and to accept a correct contact.

Above the bit

Fig. 83 Going above the bit

The horse goes hollow by dropping his back and not bringing his hind legs under him.

Causes Positional faults in the rider make the rider heavy on a horse's back. A badly-fitting saddle is an alternative reason. (See also page 113.) The rider may not be riding the horse forward to encourage him to use his back and hocks correctly.

Check the fitting of the saddle. Have the saddle seen to if it is faulty. Use a thick numnah or a gel pad. These are made from a high density silicon gel that will neither distort nor break up. Using a thick numnah or gel pad, or both, will give the horse more confidence to start using his back muscles which he had previously tried to save by going hollow. Use a mild snaffle. Ride in a forward position so that the horse can use his back muscles. When they are stronger, the rider can sit on the horse's back.

If necessary, receive help from a qualified instructor.

Grinding the teeth

When ridden, the horse frequently grinds his teeth.

Causes This is caused by nervous tension. The horse may have had a less-than-tactful rider, and may have been asked to do more than he was capable of.

Check his mouth to see that his teeth are not irritating him. Try to overcome the tension by correct and sympathetic riding.

Bridle lameness

The horse appears to be unlevel when ridden but is sound when run in hand.

Causes Stiffness or laziness in one hind leg, or the horse may have a back problem.

Have his back checked. With correct schooling, the lazy leg should strengthen and the horse's action will become level.

Leaning on the bit

The horse is very heavy on the hand and uses it as a 'fifth leg'.

Causes A horse with a thick, short neck and badly set-on head and neck, being more difficult for a rider to balance, is more likely to acquire this habit than a better put-together horse. On the rider's part, not yielding when the horse responds will make the horse take more and more support from the rider's hands.

Headshaking

This is usually seen only during spring and summer, or when a horse is very excited or nervous.

In many ways it is akin to hay fever in humans. When ridden in an indoor school the horse keeps his head still; when ridden outside the horse will start to shake his head up and down and becomes virtually impossible to ride.

It is advisable to seek help from your veterinary surgeon, who may refer the horse to a veterinary college for further investigation.

An inhaler has been known to help, as may a large handkerchief attached to the noseband and hung over the horse's nostrils. In one case a horse was helped by having a large handkerchief attached to his browband and hung down over his eyes.

Summary

- Whatever the problems with a horse's mouth, always try to find the cause. Do not simply treat the effect. Consult your veterinary surgeon, or possibly a back specialist. Books may help you to understand a problem, but there is nothing better than help from a qualified instructor.

Part 2
BRIDLES
AND SADDLES

9
NOSEBANDS, MARTINGALES AND GADGETS

Nosebands have four main functions. They may aid the action of the bit; they may alter its action; they may be used to enhance the horse's appearance, or they may be used to prevent the horse from opening his jaws in an attempt to evade the bit's action. There are many different types in general use which have a variety of effects on the horse's head.

As with bridles, the thickness of the leather must be selected to complement the size of the horse and the work he does. A well-made noseband will be correctly proportioned for its size and should have plenty of room for adjustment.

When deciding on a suitable type for your horse, first consider all the other tack you use and then give thought to your horse's way of going. Some nosebands should not be used with certain types of bits; for instance, a noseband which incorporates a chin strap should not be used in conjunction with any bit which employs the use of a curb chain. Similarly, you should not use a standing martingale with a Grakle noseband. There may be more to selecting an appropriate noseband than you first thought.

Nosebands

Cavesson noseband

Used on most bridles for appearance. A horse looks undressed without a noseband.

Fitting Allow two fingers below the projecting cheek bones, and two between the noseband and the nasal bone. Wide, padded nosebands are sometimes used in dressage competitions and fitted more tightly to prevent the horse opening his mouth too much. Cavesson nosebands can be used in all BHS and FEI competitions.

Dropped noseband

This consists of a headpiece, a small strap to go over the nose and a strap to fasten below the bit.

Fitting Fit the noseband fairly high, so that the padded strap that goes across the nose presses on the bone and not on the soft cartilage, which would irritate the horse. The other strap fastens below the snaffle: allow two fingers between

33 Correctly-fitting dropped noseband and a correctly adjusted running matingale

this strap and the horse's chin groove. This allows the horse to chew the bit, but not evade it by opening his mouth and crossing his jaws.

Action of the dropped noseband This type of noseband should only be used in conjunction with a snaffle. It prevents the horse evading the action of the snaffle by opening his mouth or crossing his jaw. It also prevents a horse from getting his tongue over the bit.

There are two schools of thought regarding the use of a dropped noseband. Some riders always put them on a young horse so that it will not learn to evade the bit. Other riders believe that the dropped noseband disguises bad horsemanship.

However, for jumping and cross country work when the horse has to cover much ground and is full of impulsion and a firm contact is needed, the dropped noseband helps by giving more control to the rider and support for the horse's lower jaw. The dropped noseband is allowed in BHS and FEI dressage competitions and BHS horse trials.

Flash noseband

Attached to the front of a cavesson nose-band, the strap drops down and fastens below the snaffle. This has largely super-seded the dropped noseband. It is more comfortable for the horse, being fixed higher up the front of his nose.

Fig. 84

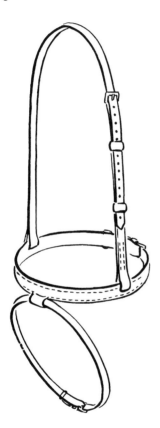

straps are adjusted above and below the snaffle. It does not irritate the horse because it is fitted high.

Fig. 85

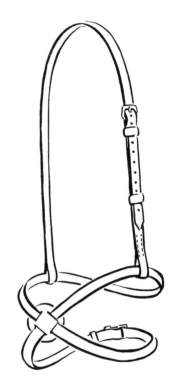

Action Similar in action to the dropped noseband. It is used a great deal in competition work for the support it gives to horse and rider. May be used in BHS dressage competitions and BHS horse trials.

Grakle or figure-of-eight noseband

This has two straps, fitted to a head-piece, which slot through a ring of leather which should be at about the height of a cavesson noseband. The

Action Prevents a horse from opening his mouth and crossing his jaw, and is more effective than a dropped noseband. Gives support to horse and rider for cross country or jumping. The Grakle is not permitted in BHS or FEI dressage competitions. It may be used for BHS horse trials.

Sheepskin noseband

A cavesson noseband covered with thick sheepskin.

Action Seen mostly in the racing world. It is designed to prevent the horse from seeing what is on the ground directly in

34 A horse being ridden in a kineton noseband

front of him – so it has the combined effect of making the horse lower his head to see better and, to some extent, preventing him from 'spooking' at shadows on the ground.

Kineton noseband

Two steel hooks attached to a headpiece with adjustable strap to go over the horse's nose. The hooks sit in between the bit rings and the horse's mouth.

Action Pressure is brought on to the nose by adjusting the strap that goes across the horse's nose. When used with a jointed snaffle it pinches the mouth and increases the nutcracker action.

While it may give more control, horses are uncomfortable in it. It is often used as a last-resort braking system.

Martingales

All true martingales serve basically the same purpose: to prevent the horse from lifting his head above an acceptable level. Some martingales do serve other purposes as well, but this is the common reason for their employment. Jumping horses wear them almost universally, in order to keep their heads low on the approach to a fence. This is not least so that the horse can actually see where he is going and what he is jumping, so that when he arrives at the fence he may be able to jump it in good style. Where a horse is trained properly he should not need the preventative action of a martingale. However, we do not live in an ideal world. Some horses are not trained properly as youngsters, and so may go through life with some tiresome habit which has to be restrained, as it is unlikely to be cured. Other horses can become excitable, so it is better to have a martingale as a back-up rather than suffer a black eye if horse thrashes his head backwards.

As with most forms of tack, there are many designs of martingale, each claiming to offer slightly different advantages over the others. However, the main distinction between martingales is whether they act together with the bit or with the noseband. When used sensibly in educated hands martingales can help in a variety of troublesome situations. However, they are not a 'cure-all' but a means to an end, and should therefore be discarded as soon as possible.

Running martingale

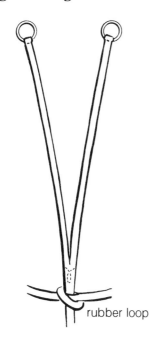

Fig. 86

rubber loop

By far the most widely-used martingale. It consists of a neck strap and a further strap from the girth, dividing after going through the neck strap, and ending in two rings. Running martingales give the rider more control should the horse raise his head above the point of balance, that is higher than his withers.

Fitting There must be stops on the reins which prevent the rings of the martingale becoming stuck on the billets (the ends of the reins) which could cause the horse to panic. The martingale should not come into action unless the horse's head comes above the angle of control.

Fig. 87 Correctly fitted running martingale

When his head is in the normal position it should not interfere with the straight line (elbow, hand, horse's mouth). If it is fitted too tightly it will have a downward pressure which the horse will resist, making him go hollow.

Fig. 88 Too tight a martingale

Action and fitting is the same as for the running martingale.

Standing martingale

A strap attached to the cavesson noseband going between the horse's forelegs to the girth, supported by a neckstrap. Some standing martingales have only the one fitting by the girth; better ones also have a fitting at the top end (as illustrated) which is much more convenient.

Having said this, to put it on more tightly for a short time, for instance for a jumping competition, will often give more control. Conversely he may fight it even more, so try this at home first. To ride always with this martingale too tightly fastened will cause the horse to develop the muscles under his neck, and he will be able to resist the rider all the more.

Bib martingale

This is a running martingale with a leather insert between the branches of the martingale. It is used mostly on young horses where there may be a danger of the horse catching hold of the strap of the martingale, which could make him panic and become highly dangerous.

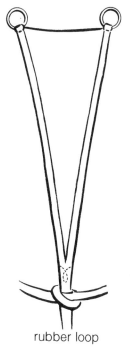

Fig. 89 rubber loop

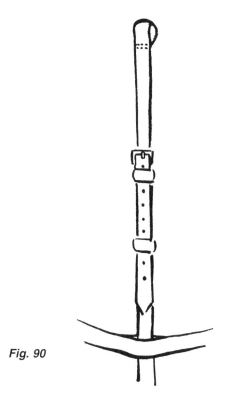

Fig. 90

Fitting When the horse's head is in the correct position and the martingale is attached at both ends, put your hand underneath the martingale and push it up into the horse's gullet. When it just goes up to the gullet the fitting is correct. Standing martingales are presently less fashionable. They are useful on young horses: if they take fright, it stops them putting their head too high and becoming difficult to control.

It can also be used for early jumping lessons. If fitted correctly, it does not interfere with the horse using his head and neck. On no account should it be used to tie the horse's head down.

Irish martingale

Fig. 91

This consists of two rings connected by a strap 10–15 cm (4–6 in) wide. The snaffle reins go through the rings. Used in racing, it keeps the reins together and prevents them going over the horse's neck. This may occur if a horse runs out at a fence, the reins flip over his outstretched head and neck, and the jockey is left with both reins on the one side: very awkward when it comes to steering.

Breastplate

The breastplate, called a hunting breastplate in the USA, helps to keep the saddle in position when the horse is being

ridden over undulating country. It is used for hunting and all cross country riding. If the saddle slipped back when the horse was being ridden up a steep incline, the result would be disastrous.

Fitting The straps are attached to the 'D's rivetted on the front of the saddle tree. These are stronger than the 'D's at the front of the saddle, which are only attached by leather.

For the neck strap to be comfortable, allow a hand's width between it and the horse's withers. The end of the breastplate goes between the horse's front legs, with the girth going through it.

Market Harborough

The strap which goes from the girth through the neck strap divides into ends with small hooks. Special reins are used in conjunction, which have small 'D's at regular intervals to which the hooks attach, having first passed through the snaffle rings.

Action and fitting The Market Harborough should be adjusted so that when the horse is going in the correct outline, he can be ridden on the ordinary

Fig. 92 Breastplate

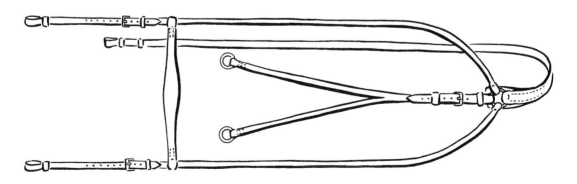

Fig. 93 Market Harborough in action with horse resisting

Fig. 94 Market Harborough with horse giving, and ordinary rein in use

rein and the extra strap comes into action only when the horse comes off the bit.

It is important that the Market Harborough is used in conjunction with leg and seat aids, otherwise the rider is only influencing the head and neck instead of the whole horse. Useful for restraining a difficult horse. Can be used for jumping and was once allowed under BSJA rules but is no longer permitted. Remember with this martingale to allow the horse as much freedom as possible during the flight of the jump.

Gadgets

In addition to the common martingales, there are various schooling aids which are referred to as 'gadgets'. This word is often used to infer that such aids are an easy option, used to gain quick results by forcing a horse into a correct outline, rather than by schooling him correctly.

This is nonsense and although gadgets do need to be used expertly, they can offer solutions to very real problems. Most of the training aids used in the UK are of French origin and were designed to correctly develop the horse's neck and back muscles, so that he could work in a pleasing outline. Far from forcing the horse into an outline, most work by allowing the horse to reward himself. If he works in an incorrect outline, then the aid will apply pressure, but if the outline is right then no pressure is felt. Thus he associates going properly with pleasure and so adopts the correct outline. However, it should be accepted that such aids are designed for experienced riders and trainers to combat particular problems with individual horses, not for inexperienced riders to try to achieve a highly schooled horse without the necessary knowledge to back it up. It is certainly true that in inexperienced hands such aids can do far more harm than good.

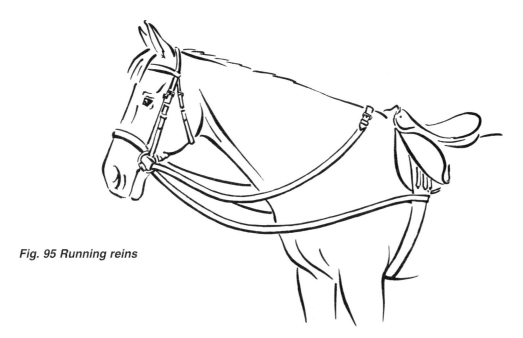

Fig. 95 Running reins

Running reins

The running rein consists of two long reins approximately 3 m (9 ft) long. They buckle together at one end and there are loops at the other end.

Action and fitting The girth straps of the saddle go through the loop of the draw rein at about knee height. The rein then goes through the snaffle, inside to outside, and then to the rider's hand. It continues on the offside through the snaffle ring, outside to inside, and so to the girth straps. It should always be used in conjunction with an ordinary pair of reins.

The correct use for the running rein is to encourage the horse to become supple in the poll, to flex laterally and to stretch down on to the bit. This running rein must be used in conjunction with driving aids, seat and legs.

If the running rein is used just to jack the front end in, it is working against all the principles of correct riding.

Draw reins

Constructed in the same way as the running rein. Can be made of leather or webbing.

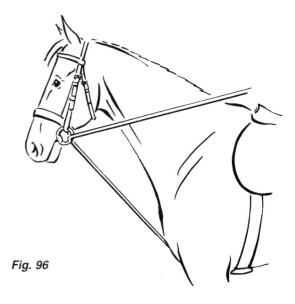

Fig. 96

Action and fitting Instead of being attached to the girth straps, the looped ends go between the horse's forelegs and

35 a A horse hollowing against the action of running reins

35 b The horse has given in the neck at about the fourth vertebra. Both this and the previous photograph show incorrect use of this rein. The horse should be ridden forward and encouraged to step under and to stretch down to seek a contact. In these photographs, he is having his head forced in; the rest of the body is not being influenced

36 Incorrect use of the draw rein. The horse's head is being pulled in, and he is taking short steps, not stepping under. If you must resort to these reins, advice on draw reins' use must be sought from a qualified instructor

fasten to the girth. An ordinary rein must always be used as well. *Riding Logic* by W. Museler explains its correct use in detail.

The chambon

Consists of two cords ending with spring clips with which to attach it to a snaffle. The cords then go up either side of the horse's face, through a pulley or loop which is attached to a strap over the horse's poll. This strap is fastened by a second, short strap to the headpiece of the bridle. The cords continue down until they are joined to an adjustable strap that goes between the horse's forelegs (through which a roller passes).

Fig. 97

Action Through its pulley action on the poll and the mouth, the horse lowers his head and neck, causing the pressure to cease. The horse regulates his balance by using his head and neck.

The chambon, through its action of lowering and stretching the neck, makes the horse readjust his balance by arching his back and raising his withers.

Fitting It is kind to teach the horse to lunge correctly or to understand loose schooling before asking him to cope with the chambon. Ideally, lunge or loose school him until he is loosened up and settled, before clipping on the chambon. Adjust it so that it acts when the horse's head becomes higher than the withers. Remember that you are making the horse use all the muscles throughout his body vigorously; therefore only work him for about 20 minutes two or three times a week. Tired muscles hurt, and too long on the chambon will do more harm than good. To fully understand the chambon, see *The Conquest of the Horse* by Yves Benoist-Gironière.

The de Gogue

This is used in conjunction with a snaffle. Rounded leather straps or cords pass through loops or pulleys that are attached to a strap over the poll. One end clips to a strap between the horse's forelegs, which is attached to a roller. The other end either returns to that strap or to the rider's hands.

Fig. 98 De Gogue: independent position

Action Similar to the chambon, but the de Gogue has two uses. It can be independent or it can be in the riding or 'command' position. It helps to overcome resistance in the poll, mouth and base of the neck.

Independent position The horse is confined in a triangle (see Fig. 98) which encourages him to lower his head and stretch down, and so to raise his withers and to round his back. The horse may be lunged or loose schooled in it. As with the chambon, it is easier for the horse if you teach him to lunge or loose school first. Being lunged in the de gogue is harder work for the horse than being loose schooled.

When the horse understands its action he may be ridden in it by attaching an ordinary rein to the snaffle.

The command position The rolled leather or cords fix at one end to a strap between the horse's legs and at the other end to the rider's hands. Do not ask too much of the horse to begin with: he must

become used to carrying the rider's weight while in this gadget.

When the horse is moving forward freely, bring in the action of the de Gogue to get the desired result. It is safe to jump the horse in this gadget.

The chambon and de Gogue, used carefully by an experienced rider, build up the correct muscles which help the horse to perform in the correct outline and use his back, both for dressage and jumping. Used with tact, thought and care they can be helpful. Force will never work. Muscles must be allowed time to develop. If stressed or overtired the horse will resist and all your work will go from bad to much worse.

These gadgets can be useful for retraining a badly schooled horse. In an ideal world a good rider should be able to school and improve a horse without them.

Bitless bridle or hackamore

See the entry in Chapter 10, page 92.

Blairs pattern

This bitless bridle has long cheeks supported at the lower end by a bar. The cheeks may be as long as 30 cm (12 in), so

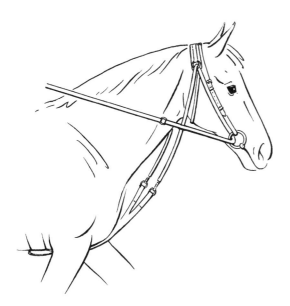

Fig. 99 De Gogue: command position

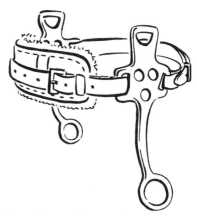

Fig. 100 Blairs Pattern (standard)

it is severe. The straps over the nose and under the chin are adjustable.

There is also a version with shorter cheeks which is therefore less severe (see Fig. 100). It works on the same principle as a bitless bridle.

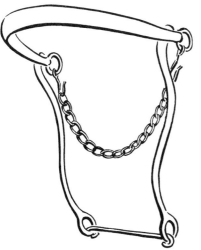

Fig. 101 Blairs Patterns (long cheeks)

Bit guards

These are round rubber rings that fit between the bit and the horse's cheeks. They can be used if a horse has tender corners to his mouth, to save him from being rubbed.

On a young horse ridden in a loose ring snaffle, they help to turn him by pressing against his cheek and also, in the case of misunderstanding on the young horse's part, prevent the snaffle being pulled through his mouth. They may also be used on a snaffle that is too wide to reduce its size until one of the correct fit is found.

They are difficult to put over the rings of a snaffle. This can be made easier by putting a loop of string over the bridle hook and through the bit guard. Pull the bit guard down: this makes it an oval shape. It is then simple to slide the snaffle ring through.

Summary

- Ensure that you understand the use of artificial aids.

- Be very careful that they are fitted correctly.

- Where possible use them constructively so that in time you depend less on them.

10
BRIDLES AND RELATED ITEMS

The three main types of bridle are the snaffle bridle, which employs one bit; the double bridle, which employs two bits, and the bitless bridle which – surprisingly? – employs no bit at all. There are variations within each group, but the overall purpose of any bridle is to offer control over the horse, either through the bit(s) which it supports, or through a nosepiece in the case of a bitless bridle. The style and type of leather-work can vary a great deal, from broad, flat straps to delicate rolled ones; this reflects personal taste rather than practical considerations.

When choosing a bridle it is important to select one that will fit your horse well. This means that all pieces are in proportion to each other and that there is plenty of room for adjustment. Most bridles come in pony, cob and full sizes, although like a pair of shoes this can vary from manufacturer to manufacturer. Again, the type of work the horse will be doing needs to be considered. If your horse is competing in endurance, for instance, he will need quite a different bridle to that required by a horse destined for the show ring.

Bridles

Always buy your bridles from a reputable saddler and get the best quality that you can afford. High-quality leather is not cheap, but properly looked after it gives years of service. Good leather is usually smoother than that of poorer quality. The stitching will be fine: up to 12 stitches to the inch. The sides of the leather will be smooth with a well-defined 'crease'. The crease is the mark near the edge of the bridle-work, made by a hot iron which sets and hardens the edge of the leather. Always look for top quality buckles.

Bridles can be bought in three colours:

London: a light tan which tones down well with use. This colour has lost its popularity.
Havana: a much darker and richer colour.
Black: becoming very popular.

BILLETS

The ends of the reins and cheek pieces are called billets.

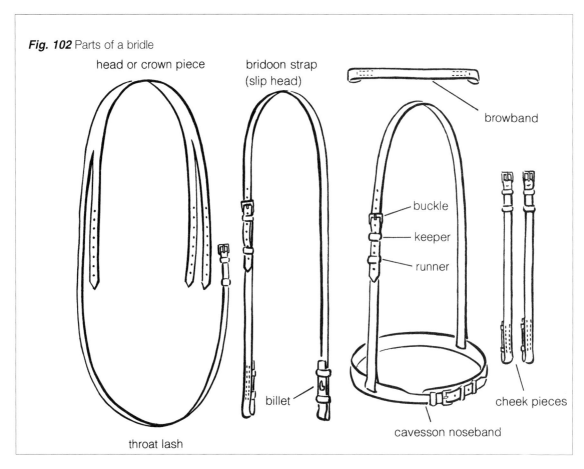

Fig. 102 Parts of a bridle

head or crown piece

bridoon strap
(slip head)

browband

buckle

keeper

runner

billet

cheek pieces

cavesson noseband

throat lash

Sewn billets Rarely used these days because of the difficulty in cleaning the bridle, and because one is unable to change the bit.

Hook stud billets These are the most usual fastenings. They are strong, and if the bridle is kept supple they are easy to unfasten for cleaning or to change the bit.

Buckles Workmanlike and not so neat as hook stud billets. Not used on show horses.

Clips Spring clips: they look neat, and are very quick and easy both to take apart and to change the bit. Used for showing, but they are not strong enough for other disciplines.

Loop billets Used only on reins. They are strong and are mostly seen on show jumpers' bridles.

REINS

There are many different types on the market.

Rubber-covered reins These give a good grip and do not slip when wet with rain or the horse's sweat. When the rubber is worn, the reins can be recovered. It is advisable when having this done to get your saddler to check

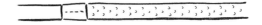

Fig. 103

37 A show hack with a neat bridle and coloured brow band

that the leather of the rein is still sound and will not break unexpectedly.

Dressage reins Rubber grips on the inside only, which give the rider grip without bulk.

Plaited nylon reins Very strong. They are inclined to stretch and to become hard; also they do not give the rider a good 'feel'. They tend to slip in the wet.

Plaited cotton cord reins (Dartnall) Soft and comfortable to use. These do not slip.

Fig. 104

38 A well-turned out show hunter. The leatherwork of the bridle is thicker than that on the hack, giving a workmanlike appearance. Note the good length of boot worn by the rider

German or Continental web reins These have leather stops at intervals along the rein to prevent slipping.

Fig. 105

Plaited leather reins These give a certain amount of grip and – if kept supple – are comfortable to use. They may slip in the wet.

Fig. 106

Laced leather reins The lacing is herringbone in design and gives grip.

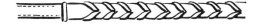

Fig. 107

Plain leather reins Very workmanlike. Their width can vary from 1.25 cm ($^1/_2$ in) up to 18 mm ($^7/_8$ in). Used on double bridles these are, however, impractical for everyday riding as they slip in the wet or when the horse sweats.

Double bridle reins It is usual to have the curb rein thinner than the bridoon rein. It is less of a handful and enables the rider to differentiate between the bridoon and curb reins.

Reins for double bridles can have rubber on the inside to prevent slipping. Being covered with rubber on only one side prevents the reins from being too clumsy to grasp.

TYPES OF BRIDLE

Which type of bridle you choose and the discipline for which it is used is a matter of preference.

Hunters Show hunter, working hunter horses and ponies have a leather bridle with a plain browband and plain cavesson noseband.

Cobs Also have a plain leather browband with a deeper plain cavesson noseband.

Show hacks, riding horses and show ponies These are usually exhibited in a narrow-width or rolled leather bridle. This group of show horses has coloured browbands and a raised, fancily-stitched cavesson noseband.

Dressage horses Black bridles are becoming popular in this discipline. The cavesson noseband is usually padded, sometimes with white leather.

Racehorses Sometimes wear coloured browbands in their owner's colours. They do not always use a noseband.

Clincher link These are browbands with brass facings, and are often used when showing stallions in hand. There are also clincher cavesson nosebands.

Nylon web bridles Nylon web bridles are now available. They are strong and

39 A neat in-hand bridle

workmanlike and can be put in the washing machine.

A variety of synthetic bridlework is available. Such bridles have sure-grip reins: these are web reins interwoven with rubber to prevent slipping. Besides bridles, martingales and other tack are manufactured in similar materials. This synthetic tack is strong and easy to clean. When cleaning it in a washing machine, put it in an old pillow case to prevent the metal buckles from damaging the machine; this applies equally to web girths, of course.

In-hand bridles These are specially-designed bridles for showing young stock and stallions in hand.

Brood mares are usually shown in a double bridle.

In-hand bridles are made from Havana leather with brass buckles for the throat lash, cheeks, noseband and bit fittings. The browband and noseband have raised fancy stitching. The leather of the cheek pieces and noseband may be flat or rolled. A rolled noseband can make a horse's nose appear over-long. (Rolled leather is used extensively for Arab showing.)

The most useful in-hand bridle to buy is one with a buckle on either side of the throat lash and either side of the nose-band. It can be fitted very correctly, and will also fit a growing young horse for longer.

Fitting an in-hand bridle   The throat lash must be a little tighter than the hand's width allowed for a riding bridle. It looks smarter and is safer because it is less likely to come off.

The noseband should be fitted two fingers below the projecting cheek bones and fastened more thightly than a riding bridle, as it looks smarter. Nothing looks worse or detracts from a horse's appearance more than an over-large and droopy noseband.

The bit may be a Tattersall ring bit, a nylon or ordinary jointed snaffle or a snaffle with fancy rings, often in the shape of a horseshoe.

In-hand bridles usually have brass chains between the bit and the lead rein. This is for strength: a coltish young horse will not be able to chew through it. The most popular type is the Newmarket chain.

Fig. 108 Newmarket chain

This has spring clips on either end to attach to the bit, with a ring in the centre for the lead rein. In-hand ponies will need only a leather coupling which is lighter but strong enough.

Make sure that your lead rein is strong enough for you to control a young horse or stallion.

Bitless bridle or hackamore   Bitless bridles, or hackamores as they are now commonly called, give the rider an altogether different feel for the horse than a snaffle. They must be used with great tact. The better the rider, the more responsive the horse in these bridles.

A bitless bridle works by pressure and leverage on the horse's nose and chin groove. The severity of the bridle depends on the length of the cheeks and the design of the nosepiece. The longer the cheek, the more severe the bridle.

Bitless bridles have great braking power when they are used correctly. Turning is more difficult. The horse needs to have a good understanding of the rider's leg and weight aids.

This bridle can be useful when a horse has a mouth injury and you still wish to work him. It can give confidence to a horse that has been badly ridden when jumping and 'jabbed' in the mouth innumerable times.

Some horses are show jumped in a bitless bridle. However, the rider must have a balanced and independent position so that he can use the bridle with tact.

If a horse has to be ridden regularly in a bitless bridle it is kind to pad the part that goes over the nose with sheepskin and possibly raise or lower the noseband a centimetre (half an inch) up or down to refresh that part of the nose that has had pressure on it.

Summary

- Buy only the best quality bridle-work.

- Narrow leather-work suits a horse with a very fine head.

- Wider leather-work for a hunter or warm-blood is more workmanlike.

11
SADDLES AND RELATED ITEMS

A saddle is not simply a piece of equipment that you sit on to make riding easier, but is a crucial element to the overall performance of both yourself and your horse. A well-made, correctly fitted saddle will enhance your horse's ability to perform in the discipline in which you compete. Similarly, such a saddle will improve your position, allowing you to stay in balance whatever the discipline. Clearly the correct type of saddle must be selected in order to achieve this. For example, a showjumping saddle will place you further forward in line with the horse's centre of gravity when jumping, while a dressage saddle will ensure you sit deep but tall with a good leg position. The overall design of a saddle is governed by the type and shape of the tree and by the angle of the head (pommel). (See page 97.)

Whichever saddle is required, the main consideration is that it is an optimum fit for both horse and rider. This means that the size of the tree and design of the panels are selected with the horse in mind, while the length of the seat is chosen to suit the rider. A poorly-fitting saddle will give rise to all sorts of problems; at best the horse may feel uncomfortable, and at worst he may

receive great pain. Additionally, if the saddle does not fit you properly either, you may have a job staying aboard your horse.

The only way to find a saddle to suit you is actually to ride in it. Though a 17-inch deep seat may suit your twin brother or sister, this is no guarantee that it will also suit you, as personal preference also comes into the equation. Often, finding a perfect fit for both horse and rider simply entails trying any and every saddle until one 'feels right'. No reputable saddler will mind you going through this purchase process; indeed a good one will insist on it. Apart from the initial outlay of buying your horse, purchasing a saddle may be your greatest investment, so take your time and choose carefully. If you are unsure about a particular saddle, then it is not the saddle for you.

The general purpose saddle

This saddle can be used for most disciplines. Try not to have the seat too deep: this makes the saddle uncomfortable when riding with a shorter stirrup for jumping or cross country riding. With a shorter length of stirrup the rider needs

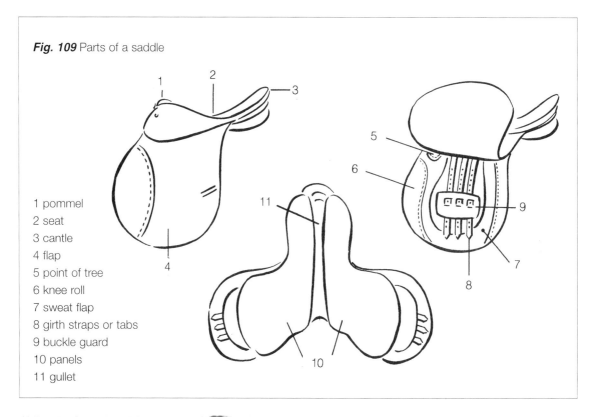

Fig. 109 Parts of a saddle

1 pommel
2 seat
3 cantle
4 flap
5 point of tree
6 knee roll
7 sweat flap
8 girth straps or tabs
9 buckle guard
10 panels
11 gullet

40 A well-designed general purpose saddle. The seat is not too deep, allowing a greater bearing surface which is comfortable for both horse and rider. Note the good clearance at the withers

to sit further back in the saddle to maintain his balance, and with a very deep seat this is impossible.

Jumping saddle

This has a more forward-cut flap. The modern tendency is to go for a slightly flatter saddle rather than an exaggerated deep seat.

Dressage saddles

These have a straight flap and a fairly deep seat. If the seat is too deep the rider is 'perched' and the bearing surface on the horse's back is small. This can lead to back problems for the horse. These saddles have two longer girth straps and a short Lonsdale girth so that there is less bulk under the rider's leg.

41 A straight-cut show saddle designed to show off a horse's shoulder to advantage

Show saddle

A well-made show saddle has a fairly straight flap and is designed to sit well behind the horse's shoulder, which gives the horse a good front and shortens his back. It is worth some trouble to find a comfortable one. The judge will be more impressed by your horse if the saddle is comfortable too. (Make sure your stirrup irons will accommodate a judge's larger – or smaller – feet.)

Long distance riding

These saddles are made specifically for the comfort of both horse and rider. Their lightweight construction helps to reduce horse fatigue. They usually have extended panels. This ensures that the weight of the rider is dispersed over as large an area as possible. Some have a quilted seat for extra rider comfort.

Fitting a saddle

To check that a saddle has been fitted correctly, first tie up the horse (unless it is a young horse unaccustomed to a saddle, in which case it should be held). Put the saddle on, without a numnah, and slide it back behind the shoulders. It should not interfere with the play of the shoulders. The tree of the saddle should fit snugly up to the side of the withers. There should be four fingers, held vertically, between the horse's withers and the front arch. If the saddle is too wide it will come down on the withers; too narrow and it will pinch the withers. The seat of the saddle should look level.

Put on a bridle and a suitable girth; then sit on the saddle. With a young horse it may be advisable to lunge it with the saddle on before you mount.

When you are in the saddle you should be able to get the fingers of one hand between the front arch and the withers, and two fingers between the back of the saddle and the horse's backbone. The saddle flaps should suit the length of your leg and the saddle should feel comfortable.

If you are in any doubt about the fit of the saddle, get your saddler or an experienced riding instructor to advise you. A new saddle will need extra stuffing after it has been used for a month or so: the sheepswool stuffing will have become compressed and the saddle may come down on the horse's withers.

Saddling up the horse

First have your horse tied up. This is good discipline for him. It allows you to saddle him in safety. Run up the stirrup irons, and if you are using a numnah fix that in place. Place the saddle well forward on the horse's withers and slide it back behind his shoulders. It must not interfere with the action of the shoulders. See that all flaps are down and not tucked up; check the offside too. If you are using a numnah, push it well up into the front arch. If it is put on flat over the withers and saddle and the rider presses on it, it will stretch tightly over the withers and is very uncomfortable for the horse. Pushing it up into the front arch prevents this. The numnah should cover a larger area than the saddle, with about one inch protruding all around.

Girthing up

Put the girth on to the first two girth straps, ensuring that the saddle sits correctly. This depends on the shape of the horse. Fixing on first and third may help the saddle to sit straight on some horses. Take care not to tighten the girth violently. Some horses will object and react explosively. Allow a couple of fingers to slide under the girth, giving the horse breathing space, and let him settle down. Tighten another hole before you lead him from the stable and again before you mount.

It is sound practice to have your saddle checked yearly by a competent saddler, who will test the tree, check the stitching and if necessary add more stuffing.

The tree

Traditionally made of beech. This has been largely superseded by the use of a beechwood laminated tree made in a mould.

Spring tree

Many saddles have a spring tree. Two strips of tempered steel go from the head to the cantle. Spring trees are more resilient and more comfortable for the rider.

· Most modern saddles have a cut-back head which allows them to fit a larger number of horses. Being cut back, they will fit a horse with high withers or one with not so high withers.

An adjustable headplate has been introduced which can be altered by means of a small tool. The great advantage of this is that it can be altered as the shape of the horse's condition alters from fat and soft to leaner and fitter.

Stirrup bars

These should be made of high-quality steel, and should always have the safety catch down. If it is up and the rider falls off, he could be dragged if his foot stays in the iron. With the safety catch down the leather will quickly come off the saddle. On some saddles there are now adjustable stirrup bars which allow the rider to choose the position which suits him best.

The leather

Most English saddles were traditionally made of leather: cowhide for the flaps; pigskin, which is thin but very strong and pliable, for the seat; and sheepskin covering some parts, such as the panels under the saddle flap. Nowadays many imported saddles are made of cowhide all over, which is specially treated to make it very soft and supple.

Much leather-work used on saddles is 'doped', that is stained to various shades of brown or black. These colours are not fast and should be cleaned carefully following the maker's instructions.

Synthetic saddles

Originally from Australia, these are becoming very popular.

Synthetic saddles have solid, moulded nylon trees. Some have an interchangeable gullet plate in three widths to ensure a good fit. These saddles are lighter than the traditional ones and easy to clean: they just need a sponge down. They are comfortable, soft and not at all slippery. They are also cheaper than leather saddles.

Looking after the saddle

Saddles are so expensive that it is well worth looking after them. Always put your saddle down where it will not be at risk. When standing it up against a wall, always put the girth between the cantle and the wall so that the leather will not be scratched. If your horse is tied up ready to be saddled, it is safe to put the saddle on the stable (stall) door, but not if the horse is loose. The horse could easily knock it off and the tree may get broken. Trees can rarely be successfully repaired.

Girths

There are many different types of girth on the market. The choice you make depends on preference and on which discipline the girth is used for.

Soft tubular webbing

Very popular girth made of soft tubular webbing, strengthened along its whole length by nylon. The buckles are attached by strong nylon webbing. They rarely rub a horse and are machine-washable and easy to keep clean.

Three-fold leather

Fig. 110 Three-fold leather girth

The folded leather has a strip of material inside its entire length. The leather will remain supple if it is oiled regularly. This type of girth is popular in the hunting field in the UK.

Balding girth

Fig. 111

Made of leather, this cross-over girth is strong and workmanlike. Being narrow at the elbow it is less likely to rub the horse than the three-fold leather girth.

Atherstone girth

Fig. 112

Made from soft leather, contoured to avoid rubbing the horse.

Tubular show girth

Made of very narrow white tubular webbing suitable only for showing.

Stirrup leathers

Made of cowhide or rawhide. The latter are very strong but are inclined to stretch.

Buy the best quality – properly looked after, they last for years. With a pair of new leathers, make sure they are changed to the opposite side of the saddle each time the saddle is cleaned. This prevents uneven stretching of the leather should one of them always take the pressure of the rider as he mounts. If the leathers are used by only one rider, the wear will always come in the same place. In this case, when the leathers get older, have your saddler move the buckle down 5 cm (2 in), to bring the wear on a different part of the leather and make them last longer. The saddler should make them level from the point end and not the buckle end, in order to keep the holes level.

Should you need more holes in the leathers, ask the saddler to do this with an oval punch. If they are holed with an ordinary leather punch the round holes may split.

Twisting stirrup leathers

Before mounting a young horse, or when you anticipate a lively ride, twist your leathers towards the back of the horse quite firmly. When you let go, the stirrup will hang in such a position that if your

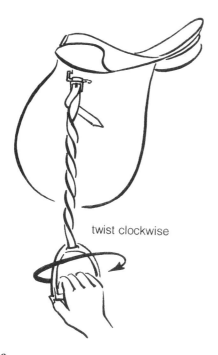

twist clockwise

Fig. 113

foot comes out of the iron, it is easy to find the iron again quickly, perhaps saving you from an involuntary dismount.

Stirrup irons

Stirrup irons are considered essential for each and every discipline. There are various types, but the main consideration for all types is safety. Their purpose is to offer support, especially should you lose your balance, but they should not be relied upon to keep you in the saddle. For most disciplines it is usual to have the ball of the foot resting on the tread, with the heel down.

Stirrup irons must be made of stainless steel. Nickel is too soft: it may bend or break unexpectedly and is therefore unsafe. Always ensure that the stirrups are the correct size. Allow 1.5 cm ($^1/_2$ in) at one side of the rider's boot. If the stirrup is too small, the rider's foot may become jammed in the iron if he parts company with the horse; too large, especially with a small child, and the foot may go right through the stirrup.

There are several specialist stirrups on the market.

Peacock safety stirrup

Fig. 114

One side of the stirrup has a strong rubber loop. If the rider falls off, the loop flips off and there is no danger of being hung up. Ideal for children.

Simplex safety stirrup

Fig. 115

This stirrup comes from Australia. It is comfortable to use and if put on correctly it is very nearly impossible to get hung up in it. The curve should be on the outside with the concave shape to the front.

Kornakoff stirrup

Fig. 116

The eye of the stirrup is offset and the tread slanting. This puts more weight on the inside of the foot and helps the rider to keep his heel down. They are marked 'Left' and 'Right'. They are very uncomfortable if they are put on the wrong way.

Bent top stirrup

Fig. 117

The top is bent so that the rider who likes to ride with his foot 'home' (with the tread under his instep) does not have the front of his ankle rubbed.

Long distance stirrups

These have the eye set in line with the correct lie of the stirrup leather. This makes them easier to find if the rider inadvertently loses the iron.

Dapps (also known as Devonshire boots)

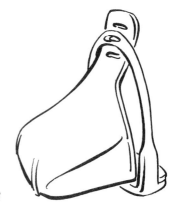

Fig. 118

Dapps are stirrup hoods which fasten on to the stirrup irons. These are used by some disabled riders, who do not have complete control of their limbs, as there is no likelihood of the foot slipping right through the stirrup iron, which would be very dangerous.

Dapps are also used by some long distance riders.

Safety stirrups

Fig. 119

These have an auto-release feature which ensures that in the event of a fall the rider is released immediately.

Stirrup treads

These add greatly to the rider's comfort and safety. They give the foot more purchase on the tread of the stirrup. In the winter they prevent the cold iron striking through to the rider's foot.

Numnahs

Numnahs, saddle cloths or blankets may be used under a saddle. It is important that the saddle fits the horse: the numnah is not there to make the saddle fit.

Numnahs make the saddle more comfortable for the horse by affording more protection for his back. Horses that have been badly ridden or ridden with an uncomfortable saddle may, when wearing a numnah, start to use their back muscles which they were previously saving.

Some horses suffer from a cold back. When he is saddled up and ridden immediately, a horse will hump his back and in some cases start bucking. Using a thick numnah and allowing the horse to stand with his saddle on for five or ten minutes before mounting will often stop him putting his back up.

Numnahs are made from natural fibres or man-made materials. Sheepswool numnahs are soft and comfortable, although in hot weather they may make the horse sweat under the saddle. The wool is woven, so that the numnah can be machine washed. Quilted cotton numnahs are very serviceable; they have a polyester or foam filling. These can also be machine washed.

Numnahs can be the shape of the saddle or square. The shaped ones have retaining straps through which the girth straps and girth pass to keep the numnah in place. Some square numnahs also have these retaining straps. The numnah must be pushed well up into the front arch of the saddle and have a good inch of material showing all the way around.

Square numnahs with a pocket for the competitor's number are becoming popular in dressage competitions.

Be careful when fitting the numnah to ensure that it is smooth under the saddle, with no wrinkles to rub the horse.

Summary

- Cherish your saddlery well. It will give years of safe, comfortable service and be a pleasure to own, and with luck it will also appreciate in value.

- It is wise to have all your saddlery stamped with your postcode, so that if

12
SIDE SADDLES

There is a renaissance in the art of riding side saddle. It is very elegant when done well. The rider must learn to sit correctly and in balance, otherwise it is very tiring for the horse and may give him a sore back.

Side saddles are heavier than astride saddles, weighing approximately 9.09 kg (20 lb).

Doeskin seats are the most comfort-able, though seats are also made of plain leather. The seat must be straight. At the turn of the century many were made with a dipped seat which was very tiring for the rider.

Pommels on modern saddles are wider and the lower pommel can be adjusted. Many saddles have two holes in the tree into which the lower pommel or 'leaping head' is screwed to suit the requirements

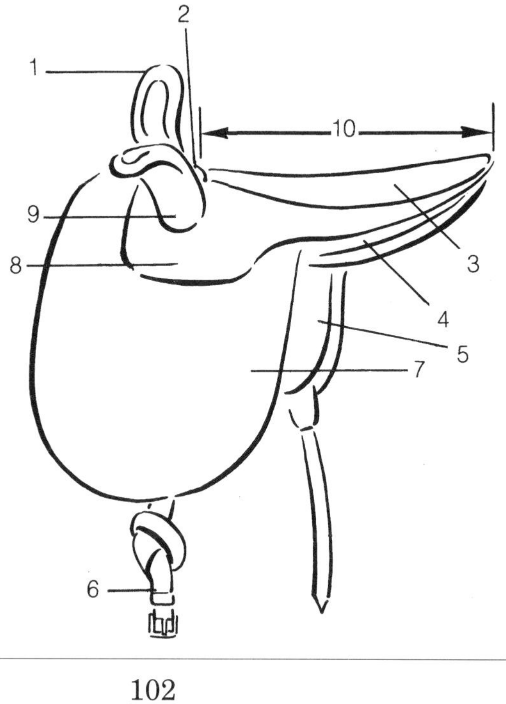

Fig. 120 Parts of a side saddle (note narrow pommel)

1 top pommel
2 cut back head
3 seat
4 panel facing
5 panel
6 surcingle
7 flap
8 skirt
9 leaping head
10 measure for size here

42 The correct way to tighten the girth of a side saddle

43 Pulling the horse's foreleg forward so that there is no chance of the girths nipping and rubbing

of different riders. Older saddles have narrower pommels which some riders prefer, because they find it easier to keep close to the saddle when jumping.

English makers of side saddles were Whippy, Owen, Mayhew and Champion & Wilton. Many examples of these are still found in good condition. An immaculate Champion & Wilton side saddle might be worth around one thousand pounds. The quality of workmanship in these saddles is superb.

To measure a side saddle for size, measure from the cut-back head to the back of the saddle (see Fig. 120). Make sure this will be wide enough for your seat.

Trees

Side saddle trees were made in three sizes, general, narrow and wide. The general fitting will suit most horses. Narrow fitting is for horses with very fine withers. Wide fittings are rare because most horses need good withers and shoulders to carry a side saddle well, whereas a horse needing a wide tree is a 'cobby' type and not so suitable for carrying a side saddle, though there are exceptions.

The trees are heavier and stronger than those on astride saddles, and the point of the tree on the nearside is much longer. Modern saddles have trees made of laminated wood and are lighter than old saddles.

Linings

Most saddles have linen linings. These are kept clean by washing all over; they soon dry out. Older saddles may have serge linings. These are cleaned by brushing with a dandy brush and, believe it or not, a good beating with a riding stick.

Fitting

Prepare the saddle by fitting all the girths to the nearside and placed across the saddle, the stirrup iron placed either between the pommels or on one of them.

Have the horse tied up, and place the saddle on the horse's back well behind the shoulder. The front arch must be clear of the withers. The panels should be evenly along the horse's back and should not touch the horse's backbone. Fasten the main girth, remembering that once the rider is up the girth can only be adjusted on the offside – so plenty of holes must be left on that side. Next, fasten the balance girth on top of the main girth, and lastly the surcingle girth. Be very careful not to do the girth up too tightly until the horse is turned to face the door, otherwise turning a horse around in a small space with a tight girth could spread the saddle tree. (This is because of the extra length of the tree on the nearside.)

Before mounting, tighten all girths and then pull the horse's forelegs forward one at a time so there is no danger of wrinkling the skin. Make sure that the two narrower girths lie on top of the wide girth and not behind it, which would pinch the horse's skin.

Summary

- Correct side saddle riding is very elegant.

- Take great care to ensure that the side saddle fits the horse correctly.

- A horse must have a good front and a strong back to carry a side saddle well.

13

CARE OF SADDLERY

Your saddlery is a major investment. Properly looked after, it will give years of service.

Saddles and bridles should be cleaned and soaped every day to keep them supple. If you are not prepared to do this, an occasional oiling will keep your leatherwork nourished.

To clean a bridle

First note which holes are being used on the cheek pieces and noseband, so that the bridle can be reassembled ready for use after cleaning, and then take it to pieces. Put the bit in a bucket of warm water. Sponge the grease and dirt off every part of the bridle. Hang the reins on the cleaning hook. Then, with a sponge or cloth, clean both sides of the reins at once. Use a certain amount of pressure to ensure that this is done easily and quickly. Do not wet the leatherwork more than you have to. After hunting, the bridle may be covered with mud and should be made fairly wet to remove the mud. Do not soap a wet bridle: dry it off either by letting it hang to dry while you do other jobs, or by using a chamois or synthetic leather. Do not put the bridle near heat to dry, as this will dry out the leather.

Dry and polish the bit. Polish the buckles.

To soap the bridle, use a sponge, dip the soap into water and then work plenty of soap on to the sponge. Work the soap well in to all the leather work. A overly-wet sponge will make the soap foam and the finish will be dull.

Reassemble the bridle by putting the browband on to the head piece, then adding the cheek pieces and noseband. Hang the head piece on the cleaning hook. Attach the bit. Put the reins on the cleaning hook and attach them to the bit. Traditionally it is correct for the buckle to be sewn on to the left rein. To put up a bridle, put the throat lash through the reins, the noseband around the cheeks, and hang it up. To make it look very neat, put the browband and noseband straight.

A quick clean

Hang the bridle on the cleaning hook, undo all runners and keepers. Wash the bridle and the bit. Soap the bridle. Put the cheek pieces back into the runners and keepers. Polish the bit.

Fig. 121 Bridles
put up correctly

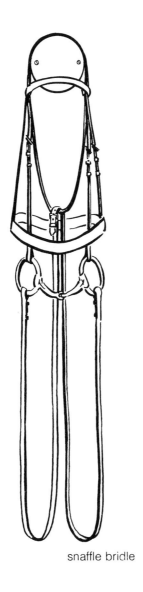

snaffle bridle

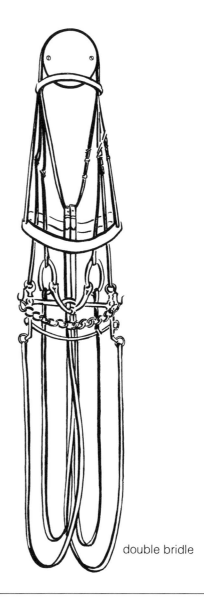

double bridle

Oiling a bridle

Clean the tack as above, and after washing apply a leather dressing with a brush. This is a quick and effective way of keeping your bridle supple. Do not oil too often or the leather becomes too flabby.

The exception to this rule is hunting tack, which frequently gets very wet and muddy and therefore requires more oil than, say, a dressage bridle.

Cleaning a saddle

Put the saddle on a 'saddle horse'. Strip off the leather, irons and girth. Hang the leathers on a cleaning hook, and the girth if it is also leather. Put the stirrup irons into a bucket of warm water. If the irons have treads, remove these and put them in the bucket.

With a damp sponge or cloth, wash the saddle all over. Sometimes you may find small lumps of grease, called jockeys.

44 Testing the front arch of a saddle to ensure that the pommel is not broken

45 Checking that the waist of the saddle is unbroken

that part of the saddle.

An easy way to put stirrup leathers back on to a saddle: have the saddle on a saddle horse. Bend the stirrup leather. Push it against the saddle just behind the stirrup bar. Keep pushing the leather against the saddle as you slide it over the bar.

Synthetic bridles, head collars, tubular web girths

These can all be put into an old pillow case and washed in a washing machine.

Buying second-hand saddlery and collectors' items

With care you can save money by buying second-hand saddlery. Most saddlers have second-hand saddlery for sale and this is the most reliable source. If you buy from a qualified, reputable saddler every item will have been checked for condition and safety.

You can buy privately or at a horse sale, of which many are held regularly in the UK, but you must be fairly knowledgeable to do this successfully.

If you decide to buy at a horse sale, arrive in plenty of time to look at the saddlery and check it over. If it is what you require and it is sound, put a ceiling on what you will bid and do not be tempted to go over this amount – otherwise you will surely get carried away and the item will no longer be a bargain. Another tip: when you have had a good look at the article, leave it alone, otherwise someone else might spot that you are keen and run you up, that is they may bid against you to force the price up. Come into the bidding as late as you dare, be strong-minded and keep to your limit.

Carefully rub these off: if you are too energetic you may spoil the dressing of the saddle. Years ago we made tiny wisps (balls) from horsehair for this task. Next wipe the seat of the saddle. Then soap the saddle all over. If there are suede inserts or seats these will have to be cleaned according to the maker's instructions.

Clean and soap the leathers and the girth. Wash and polish the stirrup irons, and wash the treads. If they are very muddy they are easier to get clean by using a small scrubbing brush.

Oiling a saddle

An occasional oil will help to keep the saddle supple. Oil the underneath parts but take care when oiling the seat. Too much oiling of the seat may spoil the dressing applied when the leather was tanned, so be very sparing with the oil on

Saddles

First of all check that it is made in England. This is usually stamped on the stirrup bar, or the maker's name may be stamped on the saddle. Continental saddles, made in mainland Europe, are also of good quality. Much poor-quality saddlery is imported from developing countries and can be unsafe due to the poor quality of the materials and bad workmanship.

Check the saddle tree Test the front arch, either by having it on a saddle horse or by holding it between your legs. Grasp the front arch with both hands and firmly feel for any give which would indicate a break at the pommel. Then hold the saddle (see photograph 45) to check whether there is any give in the waist of the saddle. A little movement may indicate a spring tree, but the fact that it has a spring tree should be stamped on the saddle under the girth straps. If the give is considerable or uneven, the tree will be broken. A broken tree can rarely be mended.

One thing to bear in mind is that a second-hand saddle may be crooked. Some riders do not realise that they ride crooked. This in time causes the saddle to be out of true. The only way to check this is by riding on the saddle. If you feel that the saddle is crooked, discard it. Nothing can be done to straighten it.

If you buy a saddle privately or at a sale, have it checked by a qualified saddler before you use it.

Bridles

Good bridles can usually be recognised by the quality of the leather. They also have high-quality buckles.

The leatherwork must not be perished.

If it is only dry and neglected, it will become supple again with regular care. To tell if the leather is perished, bend the leather and if it cracks it is unsafe. No amount of oil or soap will make it supple.

Collectibles

Many years ago loriners, or bit-makers, made bits to suit riders who had problems with their horses. Some of these bits were very barbaric. Benjamin Latchford, a well-known nineteenth-century loriner, wrote in 1883 that 'of every twenty bits I make, nineteen are for men's heads and not more than one for the horse's'.

There are still many unusual bits to be found. Farm and house sales may yield up a treasure. One comes across very old saddles and side saddles on farms. Unfortunately much collectible equipment goes to ornament public houses and clubs, but it is still great fun to go looking and sometimes to find something unique.

Summary

- Make sure that your saddle is never dropped, as this could damage the tree.

- Soap or oil all tack regularly.

- Check all stitching on the bridle and saddlery each time you clean it.

14
PROBLEMS WITH SADDLING

Many schooling problems and much poor performance stem from badly-fitting saddles, or incorrect sitting or imbalance on the part of the rider.

Fitting a saddle requires knowledge and experience. The Society of Master Saddlers and The British Equestrian Trade Association, to which many manufacturers and retailers subscribe, are both doing their best to promote this knowledge.

The greater the bearing surface of the saddle, provided the pressure is evenly distributed over the whole surface, the more comfortable the saddle will be for the horse. For this reason, troopers' army saddles had extended panels called fans, and long distance riding saddles are designed along the same lines.

Too narrow a gullet will pinch the horse's spine. The saddle will be liable to move and slip to one side or the other, causing uneven pressure, especially from the points of the tree.

Too wide a saddle will come down on the horse's withers, causing pain. The saddle will also work forward and interfere with the play of the horse's shoulders (scapula), which can rotate as much as three inches. This interference restricts his action and causes his stride to deteriorate. He will tire more quickly and may stumble.

Changes in the horse's back

You must be aware of changes that may occur to the horse's back which will affect the fitting of the saddle. For instance, a horse in big, soft condition will be leaner when he is fit. A horse that has lost condition for any reason will lose muscle tone over his back and his saddle will not fit. Also, having less muscle to cushion the saddle, he will be more prone to pressure sores. Young horses' backs alter; with correct riding, their back muscles build up, altering the shape of the back.

Pressure points

Pressure points created by a badly-fitting saddle cause a reduction in the blood supply to the muscles, resulting in muscle wastage and saddle sores. Saddle sores are first apparent in the form of soft swellings. If the cause is not removed, they will in time be rubbed raw.

How a badly-fitting saddle affects a horse's performance

Any uneven or undue pressure on the horse's back will interfere with the action of the longissimus dorsi (a pair of muscles along the horse's spine). These are the longest, the largest and the most powerful muscles in the horse's back. Acting in tandem, they extend the horse's spine. Anything which restricts the action of the longissimus dorsi will affect the horse's action and his forward motivation. He will go hollow, that is drop his back and unduly raise his head and neck, causing tenseness throughout his body. His action will be tense and choppy, which is tiring and stressful to him.

Jumping

To jump well the horse must 'bascule', that is round his back over the fence, which is one of the functions of the longissimus dorsi. A badly-fitting saddle will not only make the horse hollow, he will be unable to tuck up his front legs over the fence, but will dangle them.

Diagnosis of back problems

If you suspect that your saddle may be interfering with your horse's performance, take off the saddle and lunge or loose school your horse, both on the flat and over a fence, to see if there is an improvement.

Fig. 122 Horse using his back correctly

It is worthwhile to consult your veterinary surgeon. He will usually put you in touch with a chartered physiotherapist with whom he cooperates. A qualified chiropractor will also advise you.

How to select a high-quality, suitable saddle

Ask a successful competition rider what he or she advocates. Many now cooperate with saddlers to produce saddles that are comfortable for the horse.

The saddler should be prepared to allow riding and jumping when you are testing a saddle. When doing this, do your utmost to safeguard the saddle from rain, dirt or mud. Do not use a numnah when trying a new saddle. Be sure that your horse is clean.

Summary

- The saddle must fit the individual horse.

- The saddle must conform to the shape of the horse and not interfere with his action.

- The saddle must also fit the rider.

Fig. 123 Bascule

Part 3
HORSE AND RIDER CLOTHING

15

RIDING CLOTHES

Riding clothes need to be practical and to fit well. Nothing looks worse than clothes which are badly-fitting. Riding is a high-risk sport, so be aware of this and dress accordingly.

Hats

A hard hat is the most important piece of rider's kit. When you consider that the majority of riding accidents occur when riding for pleasure, not in competition, it makes sense to wear one at all times. Similarly, a hard hat is now often considered to be essential wear when dealing with highly-strung or young horses in the stable yard. A hard hat can certainly save your life: it may prevent a serious injury from being a fatal one, or prevent blows to the head resulting in concussion or worse.

Hats should conform to British Standards Institute (BS) 4472 or BS 6473, which meet requirements of impact, resistance and head coverage. They must fit properly with a correctly-adjusted three-point harness and chin cup. Buy your hat from a shop whose staff have completed a British Equestrian Trade Association hat-fitting

course. That way you will be sure to get expert help.

Jockey skull (BS 4472)

Silks may be worn over these, the colours depending on the competition you are competing in. Always wear one of these hats when riding on the roads. They give the greatest protection in case of an accident.

Hard hats (BS 6473)

Sometimes called hunting caps, these also need to be correctly fitted with a three-point harness and chin cup.

Bowler hats

These are still worn in the hunting field. They offer some protection but not as much as the jockey skull or hard hat. The correct way to wear a bowler is to have it resting nearly on your eyebrows, not on the back of the head.

Top hats

These are seen in the hunting field, and are also worn in some show classes and more advanced dressage competitions.

Riding jackets or coats

At one time they were always referred to as coats. Nowadays jacket is the more usual term.

If you can afford a well-cut, made-to-measure jacket, you will always feel well turned out. With care it will last for many years.

Wear a sweater when you are being fitted for a jacket or buying off the peg. You will then be sure that the jacket will fit comfortably and allow for extra layers in the winter.

Buy the best quality jacket you can afford. The cut will be better and higher-quality material hangs well.

Make sure that the sleeves are long enough. Hold your arms in the position you will put them in when riding. The coat should feel comfortable and not tight across the shoulders. Do make sure that the jacket is long enough to go over the cantle of a saddle. A over-short jacket is very unprofessional. The choice of a single or double vent in the back of the jacket is a matter of preference.

Jackets are also made from washable polyester fabric. These are useful for children. They are not as expensive as those made of woollen materials and are machine-washable.

Breeches

These come in just about every shape, colour and material. For warmth, cavalry twill is best. These can be made to measure. Modern stretch materials fit well and are comfortable, without the expense of having them made to measure.

Wash breeches according to the manu-facturer's label. Breeches with leather seats and leather on the inside of the legs have to be washed in a special preparation, available from saddlers, to keep the leather supple.

Jodphurs

These are longer than breeches and reach down to the rider's ankles. They are made of the same material as breeches.

Boots

Made-to-measure boots with their wooden trees are ideal. They are also very expensive.

There are some excellent ready-made boots available. Buy the best quality that you can afford. They will look better and with care will give years of service. When having boots made, or trying on ready-made boots, wear a thick pair of socks. Boots which are too tight are not only uncomfortable but very cold in the winter.

When new, the boots should just catch your leg behind the knee when your leg is bent. With wear the boots 'drop', that is they wrinkle at the ankle; they will then be the correct length. Boots which are too short are not correct.

Butcher boots

These are black leather boots complete with a garter strap. In the days when breeches had four buttons showing above the boot, garter straps were put between the third and fourth button. With modern stretch materials, buttons are not found on breeches and garter straps are going out of fashion.

46 A well-turned out rider

47 How not to turn up for your BHS exams!

Top boots

Black boots with brown tops, worn for hunting by gentlemen. They are also worn by show jumpers.

Synthetic riding boots

These are useful and less expensive than leather boots. They are easy to clean. However, leather boots give the rider more support and a better feel for the horse. They also give more protection.

Jodphur boots

Short brown leather boots to be worn with jodphurs. Worn mostly by children.

Care of leather boots

Put the trees into your boots as soon as you take them off. This helps to keep them in shape. If you do not have wooden trees, adjustable plastic trees are available.

If the boots are saturated with moisture, leave out the trees and instead fill them with crumpled balls of newspaper which allows the air to circulate and helps to dry the boots out. Prop the boots against a wall so that they are at an angle, to enable the sole to dry out. When they are dry, put the trees in.

To clean, sponge off all mud and grease. Apply black boot polish liberally and polish off well. Make sure that all the polish is well rubbed in and then

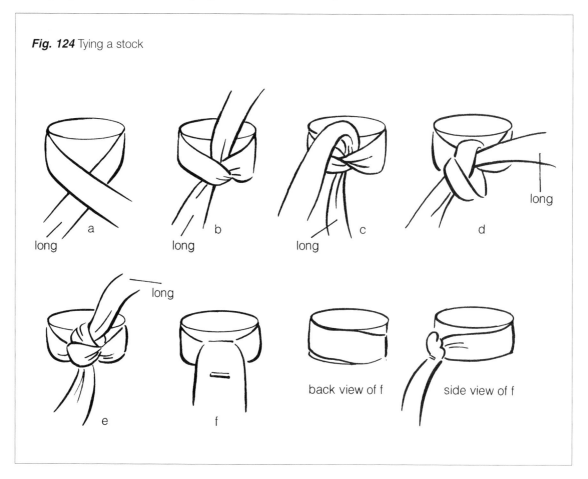

Fig. 124 Tying a stock

rubbed off, so that the black does not mark your breeches.

Synthetic boots These are sponged off and wiped. For extra shine use a spray-on furniture polish.

'Muckers'

In recent years a plastic ankle-length boot has become available. They are made with a proper heel and are safe to ride in, and are warm and comfortable.

Gloves

Riding gloves need to be generously sized. This gives the fingers more freedom to cope with reins. Woollen gloves are warm. Leather gloves, preferably unlined, give the rider a good contact and feel on the reins. Leather gloves need an application of saddle soap to keep them soft. For hunting, a spare pair of woollen gloves can be safely kept under the girth straps of the saddle.

Gloves protect the hands and should always be worn when leading a horse in hand or lunging a horse, to prevent a rope burn.

Waistcoats

These are worn under a jacket for extra warmth when hunting. They are usually yellow. They are also worn under a blue or black tail coat for advanced dressage tests.

Shirts

Ensure that you wear a shirt with a collar of the correct size, as too large a collar looks very sloppy. Hunting shirts are made of wool and have no collar, so that the stock fits correctly.

Stocks

Stocks, sometimes called hunting ties, are the correct wear for certain occasions (see Chapter 16). Tying a stock correctly is an art and needs much practice (see Fig. 124).

Spurs

Most modern spurs are 'Prince of Wales' pattern. These have a short, drooped and blunt neck. Many dressage riders use a German pattern with a longer neck. The correct position to wear spurs is on the counter of the boot.

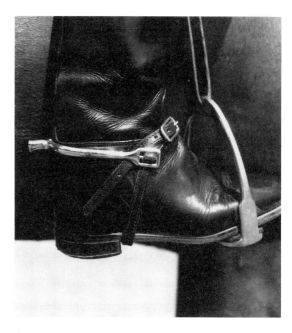

48 The correct way to wear spurs: fit them level with the 'counter' of the boot. Note that in photograph **46** they required a little more adjusting to make them level

Boot pulls

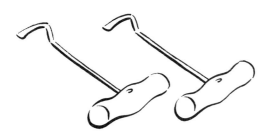

Fig. 125

These are hooks with handles. They fit into the loop on the inside of leather boots to help you pull them on. If your boots are on the tight side, talcum powder sprinkled into the boot helps them to slip on.

Boot jack

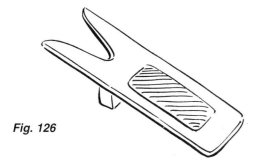

Fig. 126

Made of wood or metal. To take off your boot, put one heel into the V of the jack. Stand on the jack with your other foot and pull off your boot.

Whips

Schooling whips

These are used to support or reinforce your leg aid. The whip should be long enough to be applied behind your leg without taking your hand off the rein. The whip must feel well balanced. A button at the top end prevents it slipping right through your hand. Take care to ensure that the whip is not too pliable, otherwise it may touch the horse when you do not intend it to, which will muddle and upset him.

Racing and jumping whips

These are shorter than schooling whips. They usually have a broad leather keeper at the end which makes a noise when the whip is applied and does not cut the horse. There are several types of these whips. If the whip is too thin it is difficult to hold: choose one that feels right for you. Beginners may have a wrist loop on their whip to stop them dropping it. A more experienced rider can dispense with this loop.

Hunting whips

The horn is useful for opening gates. The metal stop can be useful to hold against the gate. The stock may be leather-covered or plaited thread. Hunt servants carry white braided whips. The thong can be held out to warn hounds to keep away from your horse. Etiquette dictates that hunting whips are never called 'crops'.

Body protectors

These are mandatory for all British Horse Society horse trials or three-day events. Candidates entering BHS examinations are encouraged to wear them for the jumping and cross country section of their examinations. The Pony Club insists that body protectors are worn for

Fig. 127 Parts of hunting whip

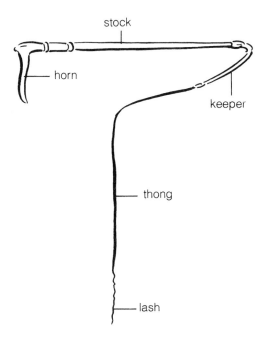

all cross country riding and for its horse trials.

There are many types of body protector on the market. Buy one carrying the BETA label. This ensures that the standard of protection reaches a tested scale of shock absorbency. It also defines the areas of the body to be covered.

Fitting is of paramount importance and a visit to a properly-trained retailer is recommended, for example one displaying the BETA safety course attendance certificate.

One thing to consider is the ease with which parts of the protector can be removed, if an accident causes cardiac arrest, to allow a first aider to use external chest compressions without having to move the patient.

Be safe, be seen

It is difficult for motorists to see a rider on a dark horse when visibility is poor. Fluorescent wear for horse and rider attracts the motorist's attention and gives him time either to slow down or to give the horse a wide berth.

For the rider, there are fluorescent vests that slip over the head. For the horse, there are fluorescent quarter sheets. Fluorescent leg bands for the horse are excellent: they show up very clearly due to the movement of the horse's legs.

It is dangerous to ride in poor light without at least one article of fluorescent wear for either horse or rider.

Tabard

When riding a young horse, wear a tabard asking motorists to 'Please slow down'.

Jewellery

Never wear earrings when riding or working with horses. They can get caught by equipment or the horse and tear your ear. The same applies to all jewellery, especially rings and necklaces.

Summary

- Make sure your clothes give you maximum protection.

- Buy high-quality clothes.

- Make sure that they fit correctly.

- Be safe, be seen: wear something fluorescent when hacking.

16
WHAT TO WEAR

Hacking

Correctly-fitting hard hat conforming to
    BS 4472 or BS 6473
Warm and tidy clothes, depending on the
    weather and circumstances
Footwear with a proper heel. Trainers
    with all-in-one sole and heel are
    unsafe. The foot may slip right
    through the stirrup iron

Cub hunting

Ladies and gentlemen

Hard hat
Tweed jacket, collar and tie
Cream or beige breeches
Brown or black boots
Gloves; carry a hunting whip

Hunting

Ladies

Hard hat or bowler hat
Black jacket, stock
Cream or beige breeches
Black boots
Gloves; carry a hunting whip

Gentlemen

Hard hat or top hat
Black jacket, stock
White breeches
Top boots
Gloves; carry a hunting whip

Horse

General purpose saddle
Numnah (optional)
Breast plate, with or without
    martingale attachment
Martingale, if necessary
    Bridle to suit the horse

Horse trials

Rider

Dressage test

Hard hat conforming to BS 4472 or
    BS 6473
Uniform or hunting dress (see above;
    some trials stipulate 'black jacket
    only')
White, cream or fawn breeches
Gloves of any colour; no whip
Spurs compulsory only in advanced
    and all FEI tests)

Show jumping
Hard hat
Uniform or hunting dress, as above
Whip

Cross country phase
Jockey skull to BS 4472 with a peaked
   cover of any colour
Sweater or shirt, usually coloured
Breeches and boots

An effective body protector
Whip

Horse

Dressage test
Novice test:
English style saddle
Flash, grakle or dropped noseband
Ordinary snaffle (see Chapter 2)

49 Horse and rider equipped for the cross-country phase of horse trials

Intermediate:
As novice, but a simple double bridle is allowed

Advanced:
As for intermediate, but a double bridle is usual
Protective boots are not allowed for dressage tests

Jumping and cross country
Type of saddle optional
Martingales, gags or bitless bridles allowed
Boots or bandages well secured
Breast plate, overgirth (which is a narrow surcingle)
Weight cloth

Show jumping

Rider

Protective headgear with retaining harness secured to the shell at more than 2 points
The British Show Jumping Association recommends a jockey skull to BS 4472 with a plain or dark-coloured peaked cover, or a riding cap to BS 6473
Collar and tie or hunting stock
Ladies may wear high-collar white show jumping shirt without tie or stock
(Polo-neck sweaters are not allowed)
Blue, black, red or green coat
White, pale yellow or fawn breeches
Black boots; gentlemen may wear top boots
Spurs are permitted; the neck must be less than 3 cm long

Horse

Saddle, style optional

Martingales, standing or running
Market Harborough reins may be used with a snaffle but not with a gag
Bitless bridles, pelhams and double bridles permitted
Flash, grakle or dropped nosebands permitted

Dressage competitions

Rider

Preliminary to advanced medium tests
Uniform, black, navy blue or tweed coat
Correctly-tied stock or shirt and tie
Hunting cap, bowler or jockey skull with a dark silk
White, cream or fawn breeches
Gloves must be worn
Boots, black or brown, or jodphur boots
Spurs at the rider's discretion
Whip of any length

Advanced tests
Uniform, tail coat, black or navy blue
Yellow waist coat
Top hat, black or navy blue
Correctly tied white or cream stock
White, cream or fawn breeches
Black boots
Spurs

Horse

Saddle, English or Continental
Saddle covers not allowed
Numnahs or saddle cloths permitted

Bridles

Preliminary or novice tests
Ordinary snaffle (see Chapter 2)
Flash, dropped or cavesson noseband
Breastplate is permitted

Bit guards, martingales, boots, side or
running reins are forbidden

Elementary to advanced medium
Ordinary snaffle or a simple double
bridle

Advanced standard
Double bridle

Polo

Rider

Polo helmet
Polo shirt
White breeches
Brown boots
Brown leather polo knee caps

Horse

General purpose or polo saddle
Bridle to suit horse
Martingales, running reins allowed
Protective bandages or boots

Endurance riding

Rider

Jockey skull with coloured silk
Polo shirt
Breeches or riding tights
'Muckers', or similar light comfortable
boot
Gloves optional

Horse

Lightweight endurance saddle
Numnah
Bridle to suit horse
Breastplate
Protective boots

Summary

- Ensure that your hat and body protector are correctly fitted.

- Conform to traditional dress: you will feel more confident.

- Prepare your clothes the day before your competition or sport. You then have time to check everything, and not forget anything essential.

17

SAFE CLOTHING FOR STABLE WORK

Stable wear must be comfortable, safe and workmanlike.

Earrings should not be worn when working with horses. It is all too easy for earrings to be caught in a head collar or bridle, resulting in a badly-torn ear. Wedding rings are safe, but rings with large stones are not suitable.

Long hair must be tied back or worn under a headscarf. It looks neater and there is less risk of catching your hair in equipment. Many workers in stable yards wear baseball caps, which looks workmanlike.

Shirts look smarter than T-shirts. Sweatshirts are very popular; many yards have their own logo on them. Sweatshirts are suitable for yard work and riding exercise or schooling.

Jeans are suitable stable wear. Riding tights are becoming fashionable, and are very comfortable both for work and for riding.

Footwear needs to be stout. Trainers do not give any protection for toes.

There are now plastic ankle-length boots available for stable wear, marketed under various names, such as 'muckers' or 'splashers'. Some have a reinforced toe cap, which is a sound safety feature. This type of boot is comfortable and

warm, and is safe to ride in.

Wellingtons are a must for wet weather, but are not safe to ride in. If you fall off they may not free themselves from the stirrup iron.

Synthetic riding boots are unsuitable for stable wear. The soles are too smooth and give no grip in muddy or icy conditions. The uppers of the boot are too thin to afford any protection should you be trodden on.

Chaps made of leather or weather-resistant material give extra warmth in winter and protection from the elements when riding out. Chaps can also be worn at horse shows to keep your breeches immaculate while you are 'riding in'.

Bodywarmers or shells (made from warm quilted material) are useful in colder weather, giving extra warmth yet allowing plenty of freedom to move about.

Quilted nylon coats are warm in winter and are comfortable to work or ride in.

Waxed cotton coats keep the rain out. The full-length styles give protection from the weather when riding. Waxed coats, even though they have a quilted lining, are not very warm. In cold weather a bodywarmer and a thick wool jersey

50 A handler dressed for leading a horse in hand, wearing a hard hat and gloves for protection. Coats should be fastened: a flapping coat may frighten a horse

will be needed underneath.

In cold weather it is permitted to work in gloves. Have several pairs so that you always have a dry pair to put on.

Ride and lead

Some stables exercise their horses by leading one horse from the ridden one. Always wear your jockey skull, suitable

129

warm clothes for riding and gloves to protect your hands.

Leading a horse in hand

Wear a jockey skull and gloves to protect your head and hands. Horses can be unpredictable. This also applies when lunging a horse.

Using electrical equipment (clipping machine or grooming machine)

Make sure that there is a contact breaker between your machine and the wall socket. This will cut off the electricity immediately in the case of a fault or an accident.

Make sure your hair is tied back or that you are wearing a headscarf or hat.

Wear an overall to protect your clothes from horsehair and dust. Have rubber boots on for safety. Wellingtons are alright, but rubber boots with toecaps are ideal.

Safety

Make certain that you never have any dangling or flapping clothing, for example a stiff plastic macintosh that may flap and frighten horses.

Summary

- Do not wear earrings when working with horses.

- Try to look clean and tidy at all times.

- When necessary, be sure to wear a hard hat and gloves.

51 Workmanlike clothes worn for exercise. Note the correct fitting of the quarter sheet on the led horse; also, that it is wearing knee boots

18
HORSE CLOTHING

Anything that the horse wears to protect him or make him more comfortable comes under the heading of horse clothing. This includes rugs, but also items such as hoods and bandages. The three main objectives of horse clothing are:

a) to keep the horse warm if his natural protection has been removed by clipping, or if he is finely bred;

b) to protect him from injury when travelling or out in the field;

c) to prevent him getting a chill if he is warm after a ride, or wet from being bathed.

Buying cheap horse clothing is a false economy. By nature, horses are a little clumsy; the odd scrape here or there will not affect them much, but a flimsy rug will soon be ripped to shreds. Additionally, if the rug does not keep the horse warm enough, he will have to eat more to compensate for the extra energy expended to maintain body temperature. A high-quality rug, providing it is well cared for (cleaned and repaired as necessary), will last for many seasons, and in the long term will cost you less.

In recent years there has been a vast improvement in the textiles used to manufacture rugs, which have many advantages over traditional fabrics. Today's textiles are permeable (breathable), where traditional ones were not; they are also easily washed – in a washing machine in most cases – whereas traditional textiles needed laborious hand-cleaning in the bath tub. New rugs are also far lighter than their predecessors, yet are far more heat retentive. With the advent of these new textiles came new designs. Gone was the need for a whole wardrobe of rugs, ranging from the day rug, through the travelling rug to the night rug. Nowadays most horses simply have a stable rug, to keep them warm and clean while stabled, and a turnout rug to keep them dry and warm while out in the field.

Another advance is that new rugs have their fasteners. Traditional rugs had to be fastened by means of a roller, which brought its own problems, such as sore backs or slipping rugs. Modern rugs either have sewn on, cross-over surcingles which put no pressure on the horse's back, or straps which go around the legs coupled with an extra-deep rug, so that it rights itself when a horse has rolled.

For many years horse clothing was very conservative, but with the advent of modern materials and designs, there is a great variety from which to choose.

Horse clothing in winter

Your horse must be kept warm in the winter. If he is cold from lack of rugs or bedding, he will lose condition. Older horses feel the cold more. 'Warm-blooded', that is quality, thoroughbred or Arab horses or those with a large proportion of thoroughbred blood, feel the cold more than the 'cold-blooded' horses, those of pony or heavy horse breeding.

A clipped or partly-clipped horse will need enough rugs to keep him warm.

Horse clothing in warm weather

Generally speaking, the warmer you keep a horse, in conjunction with correct grooming, feeding and exercise, the finer his coat will be.

Show horses are kept rugged up to help their coat. If you wish to take your horse to shows early in the year, the warmer you keep him the sooner he will get his summer coat. Conversely, at the end of the summer keeping him warm will make his summer coat last longer.

Do not keep him so warm that he sweats and is uncomfortable. He may be tempted to undress himself and tear his rugs.

Buying the correct size

Fit is very important for the comfort of the horse. Rugs are sized in three-inch increments. The measurement is taken from the centre of the horse's chest round to his quarter (see Fig. 128). Horses come in a variety of shapes and sizes. A narrow horse may take a smaller size than a cobby type with a broad back.

Discuss your requirements with a reputable retailer. Check that he will be prepared to change the rug if it does not fit your horse. It is then up to you to protect

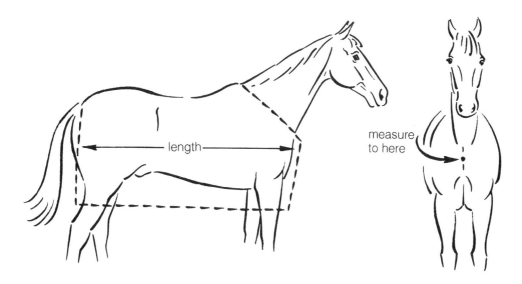

Fig. 128 How to measure a horse for a rug

the rug while you try it on your horse. Put a summer sheet on first, to protect the rug from dirt and hair. You can then return it clean to the retailer if it does not fit.

Choosing a rug

Many modern rugs are made from materials with a degree of porosity. This enables them to be put on a horse that comes in warm from exercise. The fabric allows any dampness to evaporate.

Rugs with an outer covering of nylon do not breathe. This is a disadvantage, as it does not allow sweat to evaporate. If they are put on to a sweating horse or one coming in warm from exercise, he will be unable to dry off and may 'break out' (a term used for secondary sweating).

There are also rugs with a very open weave along the horse's back and a honeycomb weave from the shoulder downwards. These are suitable to put on a hot horse to allow him to cool, or they can be used as an underblanket.

These rugs are kept in place by breast-straps and crossover surcingles.

Safety

Make sure that surcingles are correctly adjusted. They should cross in the mid-

52 A rug with crossover surcingles. Ensure that surcingles are adjusted safely and admit only a hand's width between them and the horse's belly

dle of the horse's belly and should just allow a hand held flat between the surcingle and the horse. Check the fitting regularly. Too loose is dangerous: when the horse is lying down he could get a leg caught in a loose surcingle.

Anti-sweat rugs

Anti-sweat rugs have a very open weave like a string vest. They are designed to be used under another rug. There are then pockets of air between the horse and the outer rug, allowing the horse to cool off and not be chilled. These rugs can be used for cooling a horse off quickly, if they are put on without another rug. The horse must be walked about; only to stand in one of these rugs is useless. When using one to walk a horse about, fasten the breast strap and put on a surcingle to stop the rug slipping.

Jute or night rugs

These are made of jute with a wool lining. They may have crossed surcingles or need a roller to keep them in place. If you buy this type of rug, buy it one size too large as they always shrink when washed.

Day rugs

Made of wool, they are bound with a contrasting coloured braid. They took the

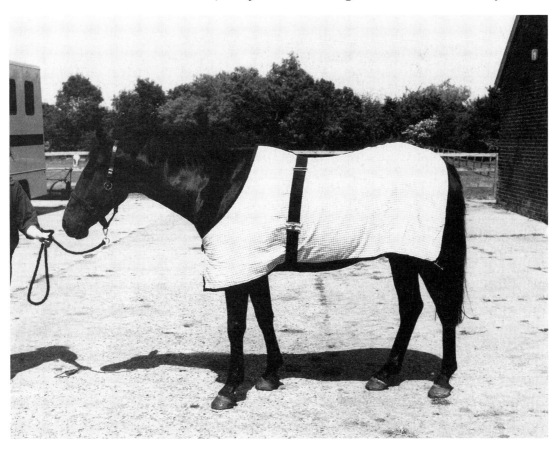

53 A horse wearing a summer sheet held in place with an elasticated surcingle. Note the fillet string, which prevents the sheet being blown over the horse's head

name 'day rug' from the time when labour was cheap and the grooms were expected to have their horses in one rug during the day, and to exchange the horses' rugs at evening stables for jute or night rugs.

Quarter sheets

Made of wool or a waterproof material, these are put on under the saddle to protect the horse's loins when exercising in cold weather.

Quarter sheets can be improvised using a day rug. Put the rug on more forward than usual. Cross the front of the rug over the horse's withers. Put on the saddle and turn the rug back over the pommel. Care should be taken that the breast straps are well forward and not under the saddle.

The reason for putting the rug on a little more forward than usual is that it is less likely to slip, whereas a greater length behind the saddle will do so.

Witney blankets

Woollen blankets, gold-coloured with horizontal black and red stripes. These are used as under-blankets. Being pure wool they are very warm. Witney blankets of this colour were originally made for the Hudson Bay Company to trade with Canadian Indians for furs.

Summer sheets

Check-patterned cotton sheets for use in warm weather. They lay the horse's coat and keep the flies off.

Fillet strings

Plaited braid, usually the same colour as day rugs. They are fastened to the back of the rug and adjusted to prevent the rug blowing off the horse's back. They must always be used on quarter sheets.

Safety

Never leave a rug of any kind on a horse with only the breast strap fastened. The rug may slip under the horse's front legs and frighten him, and it probably won't do the rug much good either. It is dangerous to lead a horse out or have him tied up outside his stable or horsebox with only the breast strap fastened. If the rug were to blow over his head he would panic, and might take off with the rug over his head, which could be disastrous.

Summary

- Ensure that your stabled horse has a correctly-fitting rug.

- In the winter keep your horse sufficiently warm.

- A rug made of breathable material is best.

- Check your horse regularly to make certain that his rug has not slipped.

19
OUTDOOR RUGS

There is a great choice of these rugs on the market, manufactured from a variety of materials. The one you decide to buy will depend on the use you wish to make of it and how much you are prepared to spend.

Most rugs are advertised as waterproof. The material may be so for some time, but the seams and stitching can let water in and, unless a waterproof hood is used, the water runs down the horse's neck and under the rug.

Self-righting rugs

These fall back into position with the movement of the horse. This type of rug has leg straps. Some self-righting rugs are made extra deep to give the horse more protection.**(54)**

Breathable materials

Breathable materials are available for some of the more expensive rugs. A water-resistant membrane is used under the outer fabric to allow sweat to pass through the fabric and evaporate. These rugs can be put on a horse who comes in warm from exercise. The more water-repellent the outer material, the less breathable it is.

Ripstop

Usually a manufactured toughened fabric, very strong and less likely to tear than canvas.

Outdoor rugs are kept in place with either one or two breast straps and leg straps: one goes around one hind leg and the second passes around the other hind leg, having been looped through the first (see Fig. 129). Some rugs have cross-over surcingles.

Fit these straps correctly by adjusting them so that the width of a hand is allowed between the leg strap and the horse's thigh. Make sure that the rug fits snugly round the horse's neck and that the rug is long enough. If it is too short and tight it will be uncomfortable for the horse.

Rugs are sold in three-inch increments. A hood attachment may be bought with some rugs. They give maximum protection.

Fig. 129 Correct fitting of leg straps

Care of the rug

If at all possible, do not turn a horse out where there is barbed-wire fencing. This can tear the strongest rug (as well as the horse). Check the straps, fittings and stitching regularly.

Use a leather dressing on the straps. If your horse lives out all the time, it is necessary to have two rugs, allowing you to take off a wet rug to dry.

At the end of the season the rug should be cleaned according to the manufacturer's instructions. If it needs to be reproofed, ask your retailer's advice on which water-repellent fluid to use. If your rug needs to be returned to the manufacturer for any reason, it must be clean and dry. Under the Health and Safety at Work Act 1972, they will be unable to service it if it is dirty.

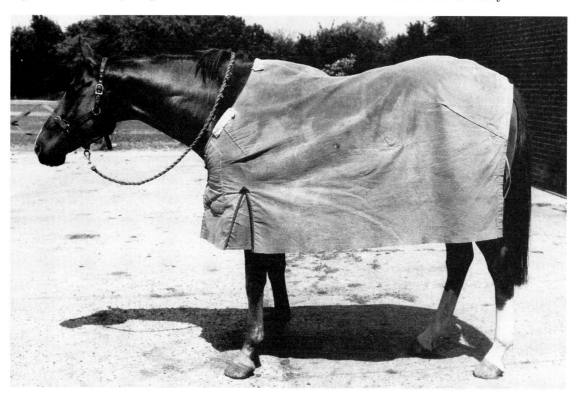

54 A self-righting New Zealand rug, giving good protection against the elements

Care of the horse wearing an outdoor rug

It must fit the horse, otherwise it may slip or rub him.

Change his rug, if very wet, for a dry one.

Visit the horse at least twice a day to check that all is well with him.

Take the rug off him on one of the visits to check him for rubs or cuts.

Do not put an outdoor rug on a wet or sweating horse unless it is of the breathable type.

Safety

If your horse has not worn an outdoor rug with leg straps, proceed carefully. A new rug may be stiff and crackly, and this in conjunction with the leg straps may frighten him. You can either fit it in his stable and let him get used to it before you release him, or lunge him and then have him held while you quietly fit the rug. Let him go out on the lunge rein and lunge him until he realises that the rug will not hurt him. If he is turned out in a waterproof rug with which he is unfamiliar he could panic and hurt himself.

If your rug is fitted with a hood, be careful that it is adjusted not to cover his eyes, and adjust it securely. As you can imagine, if it slips over his eyes he will be very frightened and very vulnerable.

Summary

- Make sure that the outdoor rug is the correct size.

- If your horse lives out all the time, you need two rugs.

- Visit a horse who lives out at least twice a day.

20
PROTECTIVE CLOTHING FOR TRAVELLING

Some horses travel very well. Others suffer considerable stress. Horses that suffer stress will get hot and their clothing must be adjusted accordingly.

Protection is needed in case the horsebox or trailer has to stop suddenly, or corners too quickly. Either of these may cause the horse to lose his balance. His vulnerable parts are his poll, if he throws his head up, and his coronets. If he loses his balance he may tread on himself. Some horses are in the habit of sitting on the tail board, so their tails must be protected.

A very smart appearance can be achieved by having travelling equipment that is all of the same colour.

Equipment required

Leather head collars

These are safer than nylon ones. If the horse panics for any reason, the leather or stitching will break. Nylon is too strong and the horse may damage himself fighting it.

If you are travelling a show horse with a plaited mane, a browband on the head collar will keep the head collar in place and stop it rubbing his beautiful plaits.

Poll guard

A sausage-shaped, padded leather piece which slips over the top of the head collar to protect the horse's poll. It is fitted to the head collar before it is put on the horse.

Protection for the horse's legs

Travelling bandages may be used over gamgee or fibergee. The gamgee or

Fig. 130 All-in-one travelling boots

fibergee must cover the coronet to protect it. As an added protection, over-reach boots may also be put on.

There are some very good travelling boots on the market. The best are those which give protection to the horse's knees and hocks and come down over his coronet. These boots are quick and easy to fit.

Knee boots/knee caps These are made of blocked leather on a rugging or leather backing. They protect the horse's knees if he stumbles when entering or leaving the transport.

Fitting The top strap should be tight

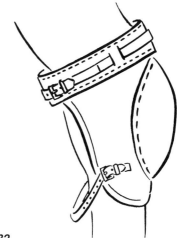

Fig. 132

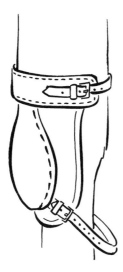

Fig. 131

enough to stop the boot from slipping over his knees. The bottom strap is loose, so that the horse is not restricted in his movement. Take off the knee boots by undoing the bottom strap first, otherwise, if the top strap is undone first, the boot will slip down the horse's leg and may frighten him.

Hock boots These are made of blocked leather over rugging. Some horses kick when travelling and these boots protect their hock. Fitting is the same as for knee boots.

Proceed carefully when fitting hock boots. The horse may not appreciate them and start kicking.

Tail bandage

This is to protect his tail, and for appearance.

Tail guard

Made of rugging or leather. This fastens to the horse's roller or surcingle and is then fastened round his tail with tapes or straps.

Rugs

Your choice of travelling rug depends on the weather, the time of year and whether the horse is a good traveller or not. Breathable material is best, for example a day rug or a cooler type of rug with an open weave.

It is wise to stop when you have been on the road for a short time to check your horse. If he is getting too hot, turn his rug back like a quarter sheet. This will keep his loins warm but allow his shoulders and neck to dry off.

55 A horse prepared for travelling. A difficult traveller may need the added protection of over-reach boots and a poll guard

Roller or surcingle

This is needed to keep the rugs in place. The tail guard should be fastened round the roller.

For more information on travelling a horse, see *Care of the Stabled Horse* by David Hamer.

Summary

- Make sure that all protective clothing is fitted correctly.

- Take into account the weather and the temperament of the horse when deciding which rug to use.

- Check your horse several times during the journey.

21
PROTECTIVE BOOTS FOR HORSES

Boots are designed to protect the horse's legs when he is being ridden, or worked in-hand.

They may be made of leather with leather strap fastenings. Modern boots are increasingly being made either from porous PVC or from neoprene rubber. These are easy to clean and have Velcro fastenings which are quick to fit. These materials mould more easily to the shape of the horse's legs, and absorb blows and concussion more effectively than leather boots.

Boots not only protect a horse's legs, they give a degree of support for ligaments and tendons.

Brushing boots

'Brushing' is a term used when a horse hits one leg with the opposite foot or shoe. The impact can be just under the knee, which is called 'speedy cutting', or lower down the leg on the fetlock joint or coronet.

Brushing is due to many factors. It may be faulty action (a horse going too close). An unfit or tired horse is more likely to brush. Young horses may brush if they are carrying and balancing an unaccustomed weight. Horses being worked on the lunge or being long reined may brush.

Fitting

The boot should extend from just below the knee or hock to just below the fetlock joint. Boots for the hind legs are usually longer than front boots, with an extra strap for security.

Boots should be firm so they do not slip or rub. Be careful with neoprene boots: they are somewhat stretchy and can be pulled too tight, which restricts the movement of tendons and ligaments.

Over-reach boots

'Over-reaching' is a term used when the horse does not get his front foot off the ground quickly enough and the hind foot on the corresponding side treads on his coronet. Heavy or deep going can be a cause, as can fatigue.

Over-reach boots are usually made of rubber. The most common boots are bell-shaped and are pulled on over the horse's hooves. There are quick-release boots, which have a tab running down through

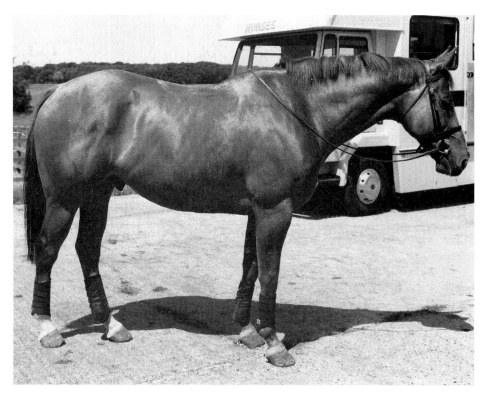

56 A horse being prepared for exercise, wearing brushing boots

two small hoops. They are quick and easy to put on.

Some boots strap on and are made of sections ('petals') of rubber which completely surround the coronet. They give good protection and spare petals are available to replace damaged ones. Their disadvantage is the noise that the petals make when the horse is in action.

Tendon boots

These are open-fronted boots that are put on the front legs of the horse. They protect the back tendons from being struck by a corresponding hind foot or shoe. Some tendon boots have extra padding on the inside to give support to tendons and ligaments.

Fetlock boots

These are small boots designed for a horse that usually only hits his fetlock joints. Suitable for schooling and hacking, they do not give enough protection for cross country riding and jumping. Used only on hind legs.

Summary

- The type of boot you purchase depends on the action of the horse and the work required of him.

- A fit horse will be less likely to damage himself.

- Always check your horse's legs for rubs when you remove his boots. Grit inside the boot can cause a rub.

22
OTHER TACK

The horse's first experience of any tack should not be a fearful one. Although most horses will accept a foal slip or headcollar while they are still young, the horse first becomes accustomed to real tack when he is being trained in-hand, in preparation for backing and riding. He will usually be fitted with a bridle, lungeing cavesson and either a breaking roller, training surcingle, or a saddle. Familiarizing the horse to these items of tack must be done gradually and carefully if he is to accept them willingly. Needless to say, if you do not have sufficient experience to do this knowledgeably, you should enlist the help of someone who has. How well a job you do at this stage will govern your horse's attitude to the fitting of tack throughout his life. Do it well and new items will be accepted as they come along; frighten your horse and you may set the scene for a lifetime of battles. What follows is a list of equipment which you may have to use at some point in order to lead, clothe or train your horse. If your horse has never been introduced to or familiar with a certain item before, proceed cautiously and one step at a time.

Rollers

Rollers are used to keep rugs in place. They are made of leather or web; leather is stronger. Rollers have padding sewn on to them to keep the leather or web off the horse's backbone. It is advisable to put another pad under the roller for the horse's comfort.

Leather rollers need to be cleaned and oiled regularly. Web rollers are more difficult to clean. They have to be scrubbed with soap and water and left to dry.

Breast girth

If your horse's roller slips back due to his conformation, it will be necessary to have a breast girth to keep the roller in place. These are made of the same material as the roller and attach to 'D' rings at the front of the roller.

Hoop-arch or anti-cast rollers

These have a steel arch that goes over the horse's back. This type of roller is designed to prevent a horse rolling right

57 A leather hoop, or anti-cast roller

over in the stable. Some horses habitually roll too near to the stable wall and get themselves cast, which means that the horse can only get up by struggling or with help. He could damage himself.

There is controversy about the use of anti-cast rollers. Chiropractors believe that this type of roller can damage a horse's back, by causing him to twist his back as he rolls.

Surcingles

Surcingles are made of webbing. Unlike a roller they have no padding. Elasticated surcingles are also available. They are often made in the same colour as horse clothing. Surcingles can be used when travelling a horse, or for keeping a sweat rug in place.

Head collars

Head collars may be made of leather, nylon web or cotton web.[Photo 58]

Leather head collars are expensive. Brass-mounted ones (head collars with brass fittings) are very smart for travelling a horse and for best occasions.

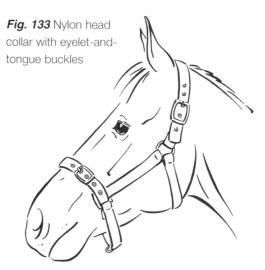

Fig. 133 Nylon head collar with eyelet-and-tongue buckles

Nylon head collars, particularly those with eyelet-and-tongue buckles, are useful for everyday use. (There are buckles where the nylon web slides through a

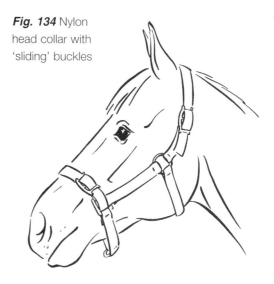

Fig. 134 Nylon head collar with 'sliding' buckles

58 A brass-mounted head collar

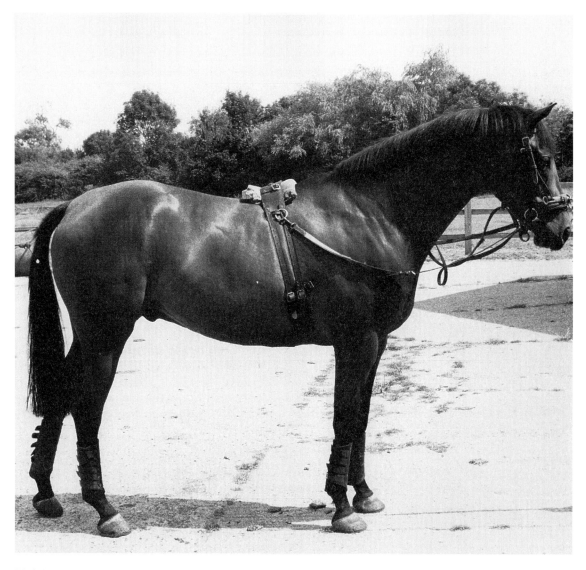

59 A horse ready for lunging. (The noseband under the lunging cavesson should have been removed.) First work the horse without the side reins or he may feel restricted and panic

type of buckle; these are cheaper but not as easy to use and have a habit of coming undone.) Nylon head collars are very strong.

In some circumstances horses have to be turned out in head collars. Leather ones or cotton web with breakable rings are the safest to use. If the horse gets caught up they will break, whereas nylon webbing will not and the horse may damage himself.

Fitting a head collar

The noseband should allow two fingers below the projecting cheek bone. Allow four fingers in front of the noseband and the horse's nasal bone. This enables the horse to eat in comfort without his head collar restricting him. Make sure that the back stay is straight.

Breaking rollers

Breaking rollers (called 'training surcingles' in the USA) may be made of leather or webbing. They are used when breaking in a young horse to familiarise him with the feeling of an object around his abdomen. These rollers have large 'D' rings at different levels. They are for attaching side reins or for long reins to be threaded through. Breaking rollers should always have a breast girth or breast plate to prevent the roller from slipping back if the youngster plays up.

Breaking or lunging cavessons

Fig. 135

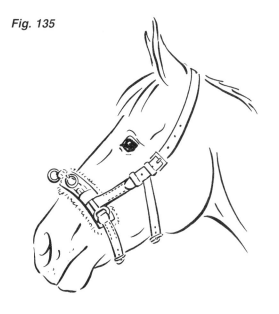

These are made of leather or nylon webbing with a triple-hinged piece of metal across the nose. There are three rings attached to the metal. The middle ring is used for lunging a horse, the side rings for long reining off the cavesson. The metal gives the cavesson strength, and gives you more control of the horse.

Fitting

The nosepiece must be half-way between the horse's projecting cheek bones and his mouth. The strap attached to the cheeks must be sufficiently tight to prevent the outer cheek being pulled over the horse's eye when he is being lunged. The bottom strap should be tight enough to control him, but loose enough for him to relax his lower jaw.

Fitting a lunge cavesson over a bridle

Remove the noseband from the bridle. It is rather bulky if left on. Fit the bridle. Put on the lunge cavesson with the noseband straps under the cheek pieces of the bridle. If you put the cavesson over the cheek straps you will interfere with the action of the bit. If the bridle still has reins, twist them several times, then thread through the throat lash and fasten. This is the safe way to do things: the horse has the freedom to use his head and back but will not be endangered by loose, dangling reins.

Side reins

Side reins are used to encourage the young horse to make contact with the bit, not by strapping his head in but, as in riding, by working the horse forward into a contact. In later schooling, side reins control the outline of the horse and help him to develop the correct muscles.

Side reins may be attached to a breaking roller or fastened to the girth straps of the saddle. The correct way to fasten them is to put the loop of the side rein around the middle girth strap of a general purpose saddle, or the last girth strap of a dressage saddle. Then the front girth

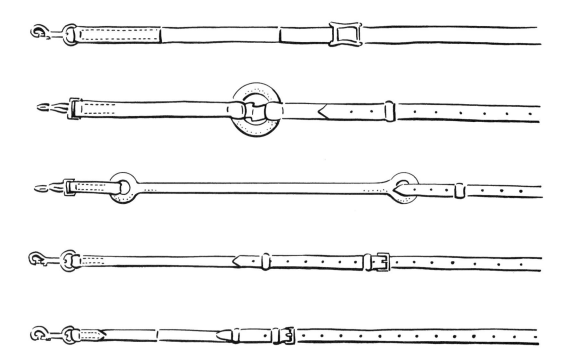

Fig. 136 Side reins in common use. Some provide a certain amount of 'give': always use the reins most appropriate to you and your horse.

strap is fastened over the side rein. This is a very secure way to attach them.

Side reins may be made of leather or nylon webbing. They have a spring clip to attach the reins to the bit. Leather side reins are more expensive than nylon webbing but they are easier to adjust. Nylon web with a slide fastening is not easy to adjust, nor to get level. Some side reins have elastic inserts, and the Continental pattern has a rubber ring insert. Some trainers like the steady contact of the ordinary side reins, while others like the give and take of rubber inserts.

Lunge reins

Lunge reins are made of tubular webbing and vary in size from 18 to 30 feet long. At one end there is a swivel billet with a spring clip and at the other there is a loop for the rider's hand.

Safety

When lunging a horse, always make certain that the rein is held in loops of the same size. If the loops become uneven and too big there is a danger that your foot may become caught in the loop.

Long reins

Long reins are made of tubular or solid webbing. Some long reins buckle together at the end.

Safety

Never long rein with the buckles fastened, for two reasons. First, if the horse gets out of control and you have to let go of a rein, it is easier to shorten the one rein and gradually get him in to you. If they are buckled together the horse can get tangled up in them. Secondly, it is all too easy to get your foot caught in the loop formed by the buckle end, which might be dangerous.

Lead ropes

Lead ropes are used for leading a horse in hand. They are made of cotton or nylon web. Cotton is easier to handle and less likely to be pulled through your hand than nylon webbing. Lead ropes have a spring clip which fastens on to the back ring of the head collar. You will have less control over your horse if your lead rope is clipped on to a side ring.

Safety

Always wear gloves when leading out a horse, either for lunging or for long reining. Not only will gloves give you more grip, but they will prevent you skinning your hand if the rope or rein is pulled through.

Summary

- Make sure that all your breaking equipment is strong and sound.

- Learn how to lunge properly and handle your equipment safely.

- Use a binder twine loop, nylon bailer twine, when tying up your horse, especially when using a nylon web head collar.

GLOSSARY

Action: the physical movement of the horse.

Action of the bit: the effect the bit has on the horse.

Aids: signals given to the horse by the rider.

Anticipation on the part of the rider: through feel the rider can anticipate what the horse may do next.

Anticipation on the part of the horse: through repetition the horse anticipates the rider's needs.

Artificial aids: whips, spurs and any tack which helps the rider to control the horse.

Banbury action: any bit in which the mouthpiece passes through the cheeks, enabling the cheeks to act independently.

Bars: the sensitive gums between the incisor teeth and the molars, on which the bit rests.

Bascule: the correct rounding of the horse's back over a jump.

Bearing surface: a surface which bears weight.

Billets: the fastenings at the end of the reins.

Breaking out: secondary sweating by the horse, due to tension or tiredness, or both.

Bone: the measurement of bone taken just below the horse's knee.

Bridle patch: the cutting of a small amount of mane to allow for an easy parting between the forelock and the mane.

Brushing: the horse hitting himself in the leg with the opposite foot or shoe.

BETA: British Equestrian Trade Association.

BHS: British Horse Society.

BSJA: British Show Jumping Association.

Cast: a horse is said to be cast when he rolls, either in the stable or the field, and afterwards finds himself unable to rise without assistance.

Collection: a horse is said to be collected when he moves with sufficient impulsion and suppleness to carry more weight on his hindquarters, lightening the forehand.

Contact: the soft, elastic connection between the horse's mouth and the rider's hands.

Collapsing: describes a rider who habitually rounds his back, which makes her heavy and unable to follow the movement of the horse.

Cooler: a porous rug used to cool down a hot horse.

Counter: the seam at the top of the foot

of a riding boot.

Crease: a line near the edge of bridlework, made by a hot iron.

Evasions: difficulties caused by the horse ignoring the rider's aids, either through disobedience, lack of understanding or inability to carry out the rider's wishes.

Evenness in the rein: when the horse takes the same amount of contact on both reins.

Fans: the extended panels on troopers' and some long distance saddles, which give a large bearing surface to the saddle, thus spreading the rider's weight over a greater area of the horse's back.

FEI: Fédération Equestre International, the governing body through which all international competitions are run.

Fillet strings: plaited braid string attached to the back of rugs to prevent them blowing up over the horse's back.

Flexions: the term used when the horse 'gives' to the reins; flexion applies to the lower jaw, the poll and the sideways movement of the head (lateral flexion).

Fly ring: the small ring in the middle of a curb chain through which the lip strap fastens.

Gamgee tissue: cotton wool covered on both sides with gauze, used under stable and travelling bandages for extra warmth and protection.

Hollow: describes a horse who has dropped his back and stiffened against the rider.

Hot horse: a very keen horse.

Hunting tie: another name for a stock. Hunting tie is generally regarded as the correct name.

Impulsion: the desire to go forward; the horse uses his loins, quarters and hind legs to propel himself forward.

Independent seat: describes the position of a rider who is well balanced, so that he is independent of the reins in order to maintain his position in the saddle.

Incisors: the front teeth of the horse (six on the lower jaw, six on the upper).

James, Fillis: a well-known 19th-century horseman.

Keepers: loops situated next to buckles on saddlery, through which straps are fastened for security.

Lateral movements: these are movements on two tracks (i.e. the horse's position causes the hoof prints to leave two separate tracks); their aim is to make the horse supple and obedient to the rider's aids.

Lateral action of the bit: the sideways movement of the bit, helping to turn the horse.

Leaping head: the lower pommel on a side saddle.

Lingual canal: the cavity in a horse's mouth in which the tongue rests.

Lip strap: the small strap to be found on a curb bit or pelham; it threads through the fly link of a curb chain to prevent the loss of the chain.

Molars: the large teeth with which the horse grinds his food.

Mount: the term for the leatherwork of a bridle.

Nappy: an evasion; e.g. a horse refusing to go forward or not turn in the required direction is being nappy.

Natural aids: the rider's legs, hands, back and distribution of weight, his voice and his eyes (to plan ahead).

Neck reining: the pressure of the outside rein against his neck that tells a horse to turn.

On the bit: a horse is 'on the bit' when he accepts the rider's hand and maintains an outline suitable for his stage of training.

Outline: the horse, through working from behind (i.e. using his hindquaters correctly), rounds his back and flexes his poll and his lower jaw.

Parrot-mouthed: a horse is said to be parrot-mouthed when his top jaw is over-shot, so that the incisors and molars on his upper jaw are in front of those on the lower jaw.

Plated: refers to a steel bit that has been chromium-plated.

Resistances: describes a horse opposing his rider; possibly due to bad riding, ill-fitting tack or lack of understanding on the part of the horse.

Rhythm: the beat of the horse's footfalls on the ground.

Ripstop: a tough material used to make waterproof rugs.

Runners: the sliding loops into which the ends of straps are tucked.

Saddle horse: (UK) the piece of equip-ment on which a saddle is placed to be cleaned.

Spurrier: a spur-maker.

Stops: the rubber lozenge on reins which prevents a running martingale ring sticking on the billets.

Tempo: the speed of the horse's rhythm.

Thoroughbred: (UK) a horse registered in the General Stud Book at Weatherbys (Wellingborough).

Trotter: a breed of horse developed for harness racing.

Weymouth: a curb or pelham bit in which the cheeks pass through the mouthpiece.

Wolf teeth: rudimentary teeth, usually found near the molars.

BIBLIOGRAPHY

Books

Doreen Archer Houblon, *Side Saddle* (Country Life, 1993)

Yves Benoist-Gironière, *The Conquest of the Horse* (Hurst & Blacket, 1952)

Hans von Blixen-Finecke, *The Art of Riding* (J. A. Allen, 1977)

Lida Fleitmann Bloodgood, *The Saddle of Queens* (J. A. Allen, 1959)

Udo Burger (trans. Nicole Bartle), *The Way to Perfect Horsemanship* (J. A. Allen, 1986)

Tricia Gardiner, *Training the Dressage Horse* (Warde Locke, 1994)

David Hamer, *Care of the Stabled Horse* (B.T. Batsford Ltd, 1993)

Elwyn Hartley Edwards, *The Saddle* (J. A. Allen, 1990)

Elwyn Hartley Edwards, *Bitting* (J. A. Allen, 1990)

Elwyn Hartley Edwards, *Training Aids* (J. A. Allen, 1990)

W Museler, *Riding Logic*

Julie Richardson, *Horse Tack* (Pelham Books, 1982)

Ulrick Schramm, *The Undisciplined Horse* (J. A. Allen, 1986)

Diana R Tuke, *Bit by Bit* (J. A. Allen, 1977)

Video

British Horse Society, *Be Safe with Horses* (AudioVisual Communications, Eire)

EQUESTRIAN SUPPLIERS AND SERVICES

British Equestrian Insurance Ltd
Hilderbook House
The Slade
Tonbridge
Kent TN9 1HY
Equestrian insurance specialists

British Equestrian Trade Association
Wothersome Grange
Bramham
Wetherby
West Yorkshire LS23 6LY
*Represents over 500 companies, all of
which subscribe to a code of conduct*

Bedford Riding Breeches
New Quebec Street
London W1H 7DG
Suppliers of riding wear

Callcutts & Sons
Sutton Scotney
Hampshire SO21 3RA
*Stockist of new and second-hand riding
boots and clothes*

Cottage Craft
Cottage Industries Ltd
Crown Lane
Wychbold
Droitwich
Worcestershire WR9 0BX
Manufacturers of equestrian equipment

Coleman Equestrian Ltd
21 High Street
Hythe
Southampton
Hants SO4 6AG
Suppliers of leather care products

Equestrian Vision
PO Box 142
Jubilee Estate
Horsham
West Sussex RH13 5FJ
Instruction videos

Herbert Johnson
30 New Bond Street
London SW1Y 9HD
Hatters

James Lock & Son
St James Street
London SW1A 1EF
Hatters

Langston & Son
42 The Pantiles
Tunbridge Wells
Kent TN2 5TN
*Suppliers of side saddles, habits and
accessories*

Lyndon-Dykes of London
6 Brewer Street
Maidstone
Kent ME14 1RU
Specialist saddlery service

Old Basing Saddlery
69 The Street
Old Basing
Basingstoke
Hampshire RG24 0BY
Saddlery and riding wear (also mail order)

P I A Associates
Tuddenham
Suffolk IP28 6TB
Manufacturers of 'Poly Pads', back protectors for horses

Ride Away Saddlery
Stillington Road
Sutton on the Forest
York YO6 1EH
Saddlery and riding-wear (also mail order)

Robinsons Retail Store
71–77 Warrington Road
Aston-in-Makerfield
Wigan
Lancashire WN4 9PJ

Robinsons Mail Order
Unit 26/27 Salisbury Road
Haydock
Merseyside WA11 9XG
Saddlery, riding-wear and horse equipment

Sandon Saddlery Company
Buntingford
Hertfordshire SG9 0QW
Saddlery and riding-wear, new and second-hand

Schnieder Boots
16 Clifford Street
New Bond Street
London W1X 1RG
Bootmakers (also mail order)

South Essex Insurance Brokers Ltd
South Essex House
South Oakendon
Essex RM15 6NU
Specialist equine insurers

Uppingham Dress Agency
2-6 Orange Street
Uppingham
Leicestershire LE15 9SQ
Second-hand boots and riding wear

Walkers
6 Bell Court Centre
Stratford-on-Avon
Warwickshire CV37 6JP
Bootmakers (also mail order)

Bernard Wetherill
8 Saville Row
London W1X 1AF
Bespoke tailor of riding coats and breeches

Wyvern Equestrian Specialist Books
Wyvern House
6 The Business Park
Ely
Cambridgeshire CB6 4JW
Equestrian book club

INDEX

Numbers in italics refer to
illustrations.

A
aids 62
 re-education to 24
action 50, 56-7
 athletic 56
 hock 56
age 58
American gag 30
anti-cast roller 145
Arab 54, 65, 92
armchair seat 61

B
balance 54-6
balding gag 30
Banbury action 39, 42, 44, 48, 66
bars 12, 54, 69
 bruising of 66
bascule 114
basic schooling 27
Baucher 22
BHS dressage competitions 18, 74,
75, 76
billets 87-8
bit
 above the 61, 70
 behind the 61, 70
 guards 86
 leaning on the 71
 metals 17
bitting
 problems 65-72
body protectors 122
bone, measuring 53
boot
 jack 122
 pulls 122

bowler hats 116
brass buckles 91
breeding 58
bridoon 40
 carrier 46
braking power 33
breaking rollers 149
breastgirth 145
breastplate 80
breeches 117
bridle
 colours 87
 cleaning 107
 lameness 71
 oiling 108
 patch 14
bridles 87, 91-2, 111
 bitless 65, 85, 87, 92
  Blairs pattern 85, 86
 double 87
 fitting 12-16
 snaffle 87
brush 57
brushing boots 143
BETA 116
BSI 116
BSJA rules 81

C
cannon bones 53
cavesson noseband 15, 41
Chambon 84, 85
Chartered physiotherapist 114
cheeks, lacerations of 66
Cheltenham gag 30
cherry rollers 36
children's ponies 35, 37, 39
chin
 groove 65, 67
 injury to 66
chiropractor 114, 146

collectibles 111
condition 58
conformation 50-4, 56
contact 12
corners of mouth 12
crookedness 62, 64
cross country 24, 25, 28, 35, 75, 80
crossing of the jaws 69
curb
 action of 41
 bits 33, 40
  Banbury action 44
  fixed cheek 44
  German 44
  globe 45
  Tom Thumb 44
  Weymouth 44
   slide cheek 42
 chain 38, 40, 47-8, 65, 66
  double link 47
  elastic 47, 66
  leather 47
  rubber guard 48
  sheepskin-covered 66
  single link 48
 groove 41

D
Dapps 100
de Gogue 84-5
direct flexion 40
divided rein 33
double
 bridle 30, 40-49, 60
  mouthpieces 42
 link curb chain 32, 47
draw reins 82, 83
Dr Bristol 24, 24
dressage 40, 49
Duncan gag 30

E
eggbutt snaffle 18, 23
electrical equipment 130
evasions 30, 67-71

F
FEI dressage competitions 18, 74, 75, 76
fetlock boots 144
fillet strings 136
flash 24
fluorescent wear 123
fly link 39, 48
forehand 56

G
gadgets 81
gags 30
girths 98
girthing up 96-7
gloves 121
grakle 24, 69
grinding the teeth 71

H
hacks 40, 49, 89
hands 60
Hanoverian 36
hard hat 116
Havana leather 91
head
    set of 54
    shaking 71
headcollar 17, 140, 146
    fitting 148-149
hollow 28
horse
    clothing 133-139
        summer 133
        winter 133
    dentist 67
horsemanship 59–64
horse's
    back 112, 113
    shoulder 50
hunting 24, 33, 39, 40, 49, 69

I
incisors 54
inhaler 71
in-hand bridle 91
    fitting 92

J
jaw, structure of 55
jewellery 123
'jockeys' 108
jockey skull 116, 129
jodhpurs 117
jointed mouthing bit 31

K
keepers 20, 69
keys 31
Kimblewick 37
    with slots 37
kind eye 58
knee boots 141
knowledge 62

L
lateral
    action 34, 36
    flexion 40
leadropes 151
leather-work 97
leg
    inside 62
    outside 62
    protection 140
length of stride 56
leverage 27, 33, 41
lesson 63
lingual canal 65
lips 65, 67
lipstraps 39, 48-9
long reins 150
Lonsdale girth 94
lower
    cheek 41
    jawbones 54
lunging
    cavesson 149
    reins 150
    safety 150

M
martingales 77-81
    bib 79
    Irish 80
    Market Harborough 80, 81
    running 41, 75, 78
    standing 41, 74, 79
molars 54
mouth 65, 84
    examination 66
    hard 69
    injuries 66
    one-sided 45, 69
    opening 69
    structure of 54
    wet 25
mouthing bits 31, 69
mouthpieces
    arch 42
    Cambridge 42
    German 42

jumping 24, 25, 28, 36, 49, 75, 77, 113
    lesson 80

    hollow 18
    serrated 36
    straight bar 42
    thick 18
    thinning 42
    with port 42

N
Newmarket chain 92
nickel 17
nose 65
nosebands 74-7
    cavesson 15, 74, 79
    dropped 74, 75
    flash 76
    grakle 74, 76
    kineton 77
    sheepskin 76
numnahs 101
nutcracker action 11, 12, 25, 26, 27, 77

O
over
    bent 28
    rein 30
overreach boots 143

P
parrot-mouthed 67
pasterns 53, 54
pelhams 32-39
    arch mouth 35, 35
    Army reversible 37, 37
    Banbury action 34
    fixed cheek 34
    half moon 35, 35
    Hartwell 35, 35
    jointed 32, 32
    Mullen mouthed 35, 35
    rubber 35
    Rugby link 34, 37
    Scamperdale 36, 36
    straight bar 36, 36
    Swales three-in-one 36, 36
    vulcanite 35, 35
perched position 61, 63
players 31
poll 40, 41, 84
    guard 140
    pressure 28, 33, 41
pressure points 112
protective clothing
    boots 143
    travelling 140

Q
qualified
    instruction 71
    saddler 111

R
rasping 67, 68
reins 61, 88-9
rein stops 78
relaxation 50
removing the bridle 17
ride and lead 129-130
rider 60
        clothing 124-127
        problems 24
        stiffness 61, 63
        unbalanced 61
riding
        boots 117-120
                care of 120-121
        jackets 117
        horses 40, 49
roller 142, 145
roundings 32, 33
running reins 82
rug
        care 138
        safety 134, 136, 139
        selection 134
        size 133
rugs 141
        anti-sweat 135
        day 135
        jute or night rug 135
        hollowing against 83
        materials 137
        quarter sheet 136
        self-righting 137
        summer sheets 136
        travelling 141
        waterproof 137
        Witney blankets 136

S
saddle
        badly-fitting 113
        care 98
        cleaning 108
        design 93
        fitting 70, 96, 106
        horse 108
        lining 106
        oiling 110
        tree testing 97, 106, 109,
110, 111
saddlery, second-hand 110
saddles 93-7, 111
        dressage 94
        general purpose 93-4
        jumping 94
        long distance 96
        show 95-6
        side 102
        synthetic 97

safety 130
safety stirrups 101
schooling 39, 40, 50, 56, 112
        whips 122
shirts 121
show
        hunters 40, 49
        ponies 40, 44, 49
side reins 149
slide mouth 34, 42
slip head 46
snaffle 10-18, 24-28, 40
        Australian loose ring 19, 20
        bit cheeks 10
        chain 27
        cheek 20, 20
        cherry roller 25, 25
        continental 27, 27, 30
        Cornish 25, 25
        'D' 20, 20
                roller mouth 25
                wire-covered 26, 26
        Dick Christian 21, 21
        double
                jointed 67
                mouth 26-7, 27
        Dr. Bristol 24, 24
        eggbutt 18, 18, 23
        Fillis 27,27
        fitting of 10-12
        flat ring 18, 18
        French link 21, 21, 24
        Fulmer 19, 20, 69
        gag 24
        German hollow mouth 18, 18
        half spoon cheek 20, 20
        hanging 22, 22, 27, 67
        horseshoe 92
        jointed 12, 92
        magenis 25, 25, 26
        mouthpieces 10
        Mullen mouth 27, 27
        nathe 22, 22
        nickel 66
        nylon 92
        racing 20, 20
        rein 33
        rubber 21, 21
        rubber-covered 20
        scorrier 25, 25
        spoon cheek 20, 20
        Sprenger 22, 22
        straight bar 12, 21, 21
        twisted 25, 26, 26
        twisted nylon 25
        vulcanite 22, 22
        Waterford 24, 24
        Wilson 26

snaffles
        action of 10-12
        allowed in competition 18-24
        measuring of 12
spring tree saddle 97
spurs 121
stable wear 128
stirrup
        bars 97
        irons 99, 100
        leathers 98, 99
        treads 101
stocks 121
straight bar mouthing bit 31
suppleness 50
surcingles 137, 146

T
tabard 123
tail
        bandage 141
        guard 141
Tattersall ring bit, 31 92
temperament 50, 57-8
tendon boots 144
thoroughbred 65
tongue 12, 18, 35, 65
        channel 65
        groove 22, 35
        injury 66
        lolling 69
        over the bit 20, 31, 75
        pressure 42
top hats 116
travelling
        bandages 140
        boots 141
trotters 20
tushes 54

U
upper cheek 41

V
veterinary surgeon 67

W
waistcoats 121
weight-carrying ability 51
Weymouth action 34
whips 122
wolf teeth 66
work clothing 12-129

X
Xenophon 7